Tenement Press 2, MMXXI
ISBN 978-1-8380200-3-3

(自由映画倶楽部)

The Liberated Film Club
Stanley Schtinter

I'm a sucker for genre-defying *What is it?* books, and this one is further enhanced as well as complicated by chronicling a London film club that's no less eccentric and transgressive in its refusal to stand still and behave reasonably or even (on occasion) coherently. This is plainly an anarchist book designed for insiders, and I'm an outsider—or maybe one could say that this is an anarchist book designed for outsiders, and we're all outsiders interested in redefining what an alleged 'inside' might consist of. ('Can it be,' Harold Rosenberg once wrote, 'that everybody is looking for a way to fit in? If so, doesn't that imply that nobody fits?') Even though I'm a former London-based civil servant (having worked in the British Film Institute's Editorial Department in 1974–77), and thanks to mischief-maker Stanley Schtinter, I was privileged to appear in two post-Liberated-Film-Club programmes at London's Close-Up in early 2020, but I'm still a Chicago-based writer who wasn't around for any of the fun and games chronicled or evoked here, and indeed, this book is the very first thing I've ever heard about them.

I'm reminded of a legendary lecture on Orson Welles announced and delivered by the great G. Cabrera Infante at the Cuban Cinematheque, which he reportedly founded or cofounded at some point during the pre-revolutionary mid-1950s, while he was still a film critic for *Carteles* calling himself G. Cain. This was also before he went on to write his remarkable novel *Three Trapped Tigers*, which celebrates and commemorates Havana during its Batista period.

It is announced that the lecture will be given in two parts, on successive weeks. An audience gathers for Part One; Cabrera Infante steps up to the podium and delivers it: 'Orson Welles is a whale.' Then he steps down.

General consternation and outrage. Due to the uproar and its spreading fallout, an even greater number of people turn up the following week. The curtains part. Cabrera Infante is nowhere to be seen or found, but in his place, there is a poster running across the entire length of the stage that says: 'Orson Welles is a butterfly.'

Whether or not this story is apocryphal—and a Cuban friend has insisted it's the unvarnished truth—it actually says more about Welles than a good many academic critical studies, not only for its metaphorical acuity but for its adroit mixture of presence and absence that replicates Welles' ways of being and sometimes not being in the world. It's especially relevant to

his *F for Fake*, which can be described simultaneously as his most public gesture and his most private one. As a longtime believer in mimetic criticism, I applaud Cabrera Infante's thoughtful provocation as well as those of Stanley Schtinter, which are in some ways equally imaginative as well as presumptuous.
    —Jonathan Rosenbaum

There are more and more curators of experimental cinema, which is great; but unfortunately still few experimental curators. Stanley Schtinter offers us a fascinating and liberating example.
    —Nicole Brenez

Stanley Schtinter confronts us with an inescapable case of "Forced Platonism": The Idea [ἰδέα], or eidos [εἶδος] and its archetype precede each and every imagistic representation (aka *le film du jour*). In other words, he has lured us into Plato's cave, but we are unable to see the shadows cast on the wall by the fire. Stanley compels us to look the other way. Blinded by the glaring, amorphous light of the projector, to our utter dismay we can only join master Socrates' cry, "Scio nescio!": I know that I know nothing!
    And so we see, the philosophical implications of The Liberated Film Club's concept are immeasurable...
    —Peter Tscherkassky

As someone who screens a great number of films every year, what the Liberated Film Club reminded me of was the missing half of every screening event: a film or any projectionable audiovisual material is only fifty-percent of the deal. The other fifty-percent is how you project it, whether facilitating the mood and the premise of the film or breaking it apart and subverting it, giving the audience the ease they might need for viewing a work of cinema or taking it away to get a more hidden message across. Stanley Schtinter practiced the 'Art of the Second Half' to perfection.
    This is a book about the allures of presentation and the forgotten art of projection as poetry. Also, it's a book on how every individual in the dark theatre having an impact on the meaning of the film. In the concept behind the Liberated Film Club the fellow seated next to us is as important as Anna Magnani up there.
    —Ehsan Khoshbakht

On the night's wonders
the white bread of days
on the linked seasons
I write your name

On each blue scrap of noon
on the pond, mouldy sun
on the lake living moon
I write your name

On the foam of the clouds
on the sweat of the storm
on the rain thick and bleak
I write your name

On every shining form
on the bells of the colours
on physical truth
I write your name

On the paths awakening
on the roads unwinding
on the crowded places
I write your name

On the lamp that is bright
on the lamp that goes dark
on my united houses
I write your name

On the fruit cut in two
on my mirror and chamber
on my bed's hollow shell
I write your name

On my fond greedy dog
on his pricked ears and paws
as clumsy as thumbs
I write your name

On my doorway's springboard
on the familiar objects
on the blest hearth fire
I write your name

On all the flesh yielded
on the foreheads of friends
on each hand that extends
I write your name

On the pane of surprise
on the lips that listen
well above the silence
I write your name

On absence, on nude
solitude on each tread
on the stair of the dead
I write your name

And by the power of a word
my life returns to me
I am born again to know you
and to name you

Liberty

—Paul Eluard, 'Liberty' (1943)

They walked vast distances, their heads full with
grammar & swallowed geographies.
They knew the skies by the lands they walked on.
Those who numbered the most solitary minds
ever known in the west.

They drank heather honeys & organic blonde!

Everything comes down to the undertaking of
extravagant research on the lips of the
incoming tides...

    —Stephen Watts, 'they came in...'

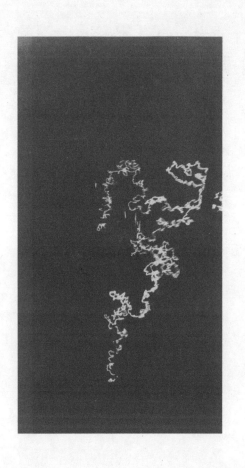

The Liberated Film Club—running from its birth to its death, 2016 to 2020—guaranteed a wide wingspan for critical conversation. Screening 'Liberated Film' (a loose category designed to scaffold the show), a guest would be invited to introduce a film; an audience seated to watch it through; but there'd be a disruption to that typical format. Neither the audience nor the guest would have any idea what film would be shown, and this anonymised arrangement would invite broad and antagonistic perambulation on the what, the why and the how of film: an interrogation of what we do when we sit in a cinema, a reckoning with the kind of posture we should assume when we frame a film for further talk. Playing with the various ways we should consider and reproach the institutions built around all of our cultures of making and the manners and methods of all of our cultures of consumption, the Liberated Film Club was a rare reflection on the act of reflection itself.

Starting out as a pirate DVD / USB company, issuing irregular mail-order catalogues of films otherwise unobtainable, the club grew into a regular event series at Close-Up Film Centre, London, curated by Stanley Schtinter. This anthology is a complete and unabridged collation of these introductions from the onset of the Club to its end.

THEN (MMXVI)

NOW (MMXIX / MMXX)

To the Liberated Film reader—

The first Liberated Film Club book was published in an edition of fifty copies, documenting the 2016 season at Close-Up Film Centre (herein titled THEN). The introduction I wrote for that book is repeated in this edition, with an addendum detailing how that book was paid for (by way of introduction to part two, and the resumption of LFC in 2019, herein titled NOW).

Best dreams—
    s.s.

Introduce Nothing (MMXVI)

(A)

You can remove all elements from an image but remove the light and it is lost. So it is that the great majority of films comprising the ongoing programme of the Liberated Film Club have been left in the dark. Cinema lost, suppressed, impossible: this is our domain.

I have spent and continue to spend TIME trying to uncover the hidden cultural lineages, searching for the key—or dare I say 'true'—image, and for its potential to undo the dominant narrative. A summary of events which led to the first season of Liberated Film best explores the underscore of the Liberated Film Club, and 'light' best describes the moments and people central to its being.

Light (1)

To experience the films of Bela Tarr is to investigate every person
he has ever worked with, and so discover *Twilight*, a film directed
by György Fehér. *Twilight* is not related to the steamy nec-rom-
com of the same name but based on Friedrich Dürrenmatt's
The Pledge: Requiem for The Detective Novel, published to reaffirm
his original screenplay for the 1958 film, *It Happened in Broad
Daylight*. Dürrenmatt felt betrayed by the decision of the producers to change the film's ending: the detective bravely solves the
murder at the centre of the narrative, rather than disintegrate
a feckless old man.

Sean Penn later adapted the 1958 film but chose to con-
clude vaguely according to Dürrenmatt (*The Pledge*, 2001). As
a result, arguments on the legal rights or ownership of the story
prevent Fehér's film from being screened in public. A degraded
transfer is now available online, but back then the film was
completely unavailable.

Through the determined disobedience of an individual at
the Hungarian National Film Archive, I was able to get a restored
copy of *Twilight* for the first Liberated Film event.* *Passion*,
Fehér's adaptation of James M. Cain's *The Postman Always Rings
Twice*, arrived shortly after.

---

*The institution at the administrative level tends to consist of jobsworths
and dullards, made worse by a leftist pretense: here's looking at you,
British Film Institute. But there have always been and will always be those
on the ground willing to fiddle the bureaucracy, for love of the work and
a sense of what's at stake. Find them.

Light (2)

Independent publisher, Test Centre, invited me as purge.xxx (anti-record label / anti-everything) and five others to curate a space in a building formerly occupied by Stoke Newington's Sea Cadets. Will Shutes & Jess Chandler—proprietors of the banner T.C.—haemorrhaged mystery money on a handful of impossible imaginations. Under the cast of Hackney's Sirius, Iain Sinclair, they hosted the final public reading of the poet Lee Harwood. They hosted Chris Petit, a car-boot full of his first edition novels and a shotgun. Stewart Home, a bag full of shopping bags and a collection of staple guns. And after the guns, the powder paint explosion of Thurston Moore and Eva Prinz's Ecstatic Peace Library: a riff on 'the good terrorists' of N16. But my highlight— my light of lights—was a borrowed Magyar Vizsla, Vigo, who led me away from the venue to the promise of red sauce and hot potato. A woman enters the chip shop after us and produces a huge wallet full of pirated discs. 'You wan' DVD?' *I wan' liberty!*

Shutes had already encouraged me to produce a catalogue of titles as the Liberated Film collection developed. I was unsure about how to distribute the work. At the time of LFC's conception the Internet was already experiencing its first great depression, so uploading the films online wasn't an option.** The woman at the chip shop gave a smart angle.

The first catalogue was distributed through purge.xxx and Test Centre's clandestine auxiliary, the not-for-sale cult magazine *Pillow Talk*. The revenue generated from our subscribers was used to produce more DVDs, which I would give in gratis to pirate DVD vendors across London. These vendors would in turn gift a random Liberated Film disc 'free' with the mainstream features their clients bought. An unlikely network developed. By the third batch, a popular rapper from Peckham was dedicated to the fairytales of Czechoslovakia—Karel Kachyna's *Little Mermaid*, Václav Vorlíček's *Cinderella*, Juraj Herz's *Beauty and the Beast*, etc. 'There's something they have the American's haven't.'

**Today, as in the case of *Twilight*, and much of the Iron Curtain fairytale fun, clips and entire films have been uploaded.

However essential this accessibility, the argument for it too often precludes the journey, as an activity available to only a few. This is untrue. It is in the physicality of things, or in the 'going' that discovery and accident and revelation are made more possible. Ideas to the contrary service the narrowing of the spaces we're able to access outside and in.

Light (3)

Behold! The insidious rot of a culture defined by a fear of the unknown is *not* all-pervasive. Close-Up in this moment exists to forge an illuminating cut across, and route beyond, the cultural deficit.

The first Liberated Film programme was conceived and constructed to mark Close-Up's first year of operation at the Sclater Street site.*** Nobody knew the film screening on any given night: not the audience, nor the speaker invited to introduce it. I produced a short text to tease / misguide the viewer, and each event began with the playback of a recording I sent from Paris which introduced the introducer ('Interruptions of The Man at The Next Table'). To compare the three elements of interruption, introduction and Liberated Film is to uncover some extraordinary collisions. And in the spirit of exposure, an edition (×3) of the first Liberated Film Club book was available with an A2 print of me—your absent host—nude beneath a scratch-able surface.

The final question to posit is which image—if any—rises to prominence; why, and what makes the image definitive? And if an image, a film, has not been considered or absorbed by the culture, are we entitled to resign it to a history? To reassess our notion of what or where the contemporary is, brings us closer to the 'true' image; closer to identifying a form for ALL time; bringing light to moments, movements and perspectives we've missed or overlooked (and where we might go next).

Liberated Film is a purge, a banner, a bumper sticker; a dogma-free deity in each and every instance. The more present we hold it, the more likely it becomes to realise not 'a life in film', but *a film in life*. And in that liberation: *light*.

***Around the corner from its original home as a film rental store on Brick Lane, a site thereafter occupied by the Cereal Killer Cafe—the locale's famous murderer of women, Jack, finds his true legacy in bowls of breakfast cereal at 6.95 upwards—fortuitously closed forever by 2020's plague. In its stead, your best bet for a bowl or a blade or a gilded brick through the window is at 'Jack the Chipper', deserving at the meeting of Brick Lane and Whitechapel High Street. First though—take care—ready your getaway and fill up on grub at Damascu Bite (119–121 Brick Lane), the maker of the best wrap in London!

Introduce Everything (MMXIX)

In 2019 the format is adopted as a monthly event: guest introduction; short and feature. All unknown. Sometime between
the 2016 season and the return of the Liberated Film Club in Jan-
uary 2019, the nationalist organisation I pissed on only *a little*
(but from great height) in my original introduction, thought it
would be good to simulate LFC. This is a fact which contributed
in no small part to the resurgence of the Club, along-with the
increasing predictability of all things outside of it: the local and
the global light fading fast; the subsequent need for a frequent
forum fixed by the question and the promise: 'See the cliff?
Jump off.'

My first introduction overlooked something important,
or at least what everyone wants to know (and nobody ever asks
about): the sheer unremitting darkness (the money). This addendum intends to introduce the complete volume by explaining
how the first book was paid for.

> With two weeks to go until the launch event, there
> were no means individually or collectively to fund
> the book's production. I know lots of poor people,
> and lots more who pretend to be poor. I know one
> or two who are honest about their finances: one
> is Gabriela, endlessly generous, practical, engaged...
> she called (at that moment from Portugal) and told
> me to 'speak.' A video editor, she was in the studio
> exasperated by producers warring over whose voice
> from limited options was 'right' for the recorded
> introduction to Barack Obama's appearance at the
> Climate Change Leadership Summit (then soon to
> take place in Porto). One producer hated my voice.
> The other liked it. They met in the middle by asking
> me to be 'a bit more Morgan Freeman.' I was lower,
> calmer, and tried to be American. It didn't work but
> it did enough: accepted by the producers and cleared
> by Obama's people, I got the job. I was paid imme-
> diately. And so, I put this to you: Barack Obama is
> responsible for the production of the first Liberated
> Film Club book. And he paid for more: the giant,
> nude scratch card of me—bloated nymph in the
> wild environs of lowest Clapton—was produced to

substitute the fact that we originally wanted the entire first book to be a bound set of scratch cards (it was too expensive and, anyway, looked crap). At the book's launch event attendees would pay per scratch, building on Barack's investment; this would generate an absolute fortune, funding innumerable future Liberated Film editions! Suffice to say, nobody scratched. But Dominic Jaeckle—of the Hotel then and today of the Tenement—responded forcefully to the overall concept and to the idea of a complete volume... cue the much more familiar unpaid work and lots and lots of it (for him, mainly), and VOILA. In hand. Salut, Jingle Jaeckle. It's not dark yet.

The first programme was dedicated to John Krish, the great documentarian who refused to confuse truth with cinema; he continues. Additional dedications should be made to those who are named or feature here and have since left us: Stuart Christie, Tony Garnett, David Graeber. Thanks to the kindness and artistry of Lijana Siuchina; the smooth of Vigo; and the beacon and the shelter and the key of Gareth Evans (for it was HE who delivered so many of these contributors into the dark). Thanks to Damien and Oliver at Close-Up for letting me and us be free; thanks to Jake, Jessie, Cara, Kamil, Katie and Jon for letting me and us be even freer. HUGE thanks to all of the guests who have attended and contributed to this book, and thanks to YOU the audience, not least those who have titled their messages to me 'END TIMES HEALING' and attached a favourite image of fire. This book is for Louis Benassi: Liberated Film-maker. 'For His Example,' for his light.

THEN (MMXVI)

Because you're sick of knowing exactly what you're going to get and you're sick when you get it.

The Face on the Cutting Room Floor
(Appropriate Everything Double Bill)
Shezad Dawood

1. If a bush can say 'I am the Truth' so can a man. An experiment in disappearance and smear.

2. The past remains present to the future... the future is already present to the past. If Jack's great undoing at the Overlook had been recorded on LSD *in 3D by* HAL 90000000.

STANLEY SCHTINTER: [in media res] ... it is the role of the audience to make the thing sail.

DAMIEN SANVILLE: Tonight?

SS: Every night, daddy! Beginning now.

Please welcome Shezad Dawood.

SHEZAD DAWOOD: At the beginning I wasn't sure if I was Thomas Paine in the wrong revolution. Some of you know what I'm talking about. This is a palace coup, and what a great palace to do it in. It is an honour to witness the first anniversary of Close-Up and to launch the Liberated Film Club. Thank you both. Should I sit?

DS: Let's sit.

SD: There is a liberation in a month of... who knows what, and my education is that of an obsessive amateur. There is something about that which we often forget: the history of cinema is riddled with people accidentally stepping onto the set of another director and going on to become the director who then re-shapes the moment.
    A lot of my film work is improvised. I'm often re-writing dialogue five minutes before an actor has to deliver it. Schtinter asked me to respond to a statement by Stavros Tornes, the Greek director and actor, and I've been trying to fucking memorise it for the last couple of days. I can't. I'm afraid I have to read it out...

Film is the liberating application
in the margins in search of a proper world.

It's annoying when someone sends you a statement like this
to respond to, because you get lost down the rabbit hole of the
statement rather than all of the other things you thought would
be interesting to talk about. But this idea of film as something
existing in the margins: my filmic education was in much scuzz-
ier cinemas than this one. Growing up in Hammersmith, I
would skip school and go to the Electric Cinema before it was
a member's club; when it was actually you and a couple of
tramps watching a Walerian Borowczyk double bill in the middle
of the afternoon, and then when the horses started fucking one
tramp would start doing something to the other and... is that
maybe something about where obsessive amateurism comes
from? Called to mind is the Nouvelle Vague: film critics thinking
'let's have a go.' Cinema is people thinking let's have a go. Rather
than this being a democratisation of space—I'm dubious about
democracy—liberation is better, and in liberation is transgres-
sion. Beyond the film itself, the site of film is vital, and so 'let's
have a go' extends way beyond the film. It is opening a cinema;
getting up to speak; putting out amazing work; taking action.

Beyond the Electric Cinema, and a few other places, we had
piracy. In the 80s, piracy was what you strove for. I had a guy in
Manchester who ran a network: I'd get one VHS tape through
the mail each week. I remember receiving *Zabriskie Point*, which
had been buried for years due to copyright issues. Film then
was much harder to come by than it is today, and there was
something about that search, about that action. I'm not being
nostalgic. There clearly is still a mode of resistance in film and
possibilities inherent in and of film, because if there wasn't, I
wouldn't be here tonight. The possibilities might be as simple as
getting a few friends together, and on twenty quid doing something transgressive (upsetting your neighbours at the very least).

But that seems to connect with this archive of all of
the films that were never made, which I fantasise about often.
Whether it's Stavros Tornes' *Robinson Crusoe*, which he was
trying to raise a measly amount of money from the Greek Film
Institute for at the time of his death, or Derek Jarman. Jarman's
diary from the making of *The Last of England* is a truly bleak
read. It's funny because Jarman now is canonised by the BFI
and Channel 4 and he hated the fucking lot of them. The vitriol
directed specifically at those two institutions occurs almost
every three pages. It's important to remember that we are
acting against. We should be at best double agents; better still

a double agent and a pirate and remembering that this is a good thing.

I won't be scathing or name anyone, but I go to a lot of dinner parties with people I'm ethically probably quite far removed from. I go to them to find funding for whatever crazy-ass project I have lined up next. Is that ethically dubious? Or is it more ethically dubious not to make the damn thing?

In a more problematised situation we need to be not just double agents but triple agents, quadruple agents: MAKE THE WORK. That's what I mean to say, and that's the point to end and to begin. I really don't know what we're going to see tonight, and I'm glad because I hoped and hope in acknowledging the importance of risk-taking, that everything I have said might look really, really dumb based on the film.

Thank you all for being here and for listening.

ss: Thank you, Shezad. And very briefly, in that spirit of not knowing, I want to quote Roy Hodgson, who today appeared at a press conference and said... 'I don't know what I'm doing here.' I identify with that because I don't really watch films. At core I am a song and dance man. I fell in love once and I showered this person in song, and when I lost this person, I lost the song. But in light of recent events, for Roy, for piracy, to begin to reunite our divided Britain in this very room. To embrace the time of the flood, to swim, for love of Shez, make the work, use your voice; the lyrics will be up on the screen.

Please join in.

sd: Can I go for a smoke?

ss: You can actually smoke in here tonight.

Why does the sun go on shining?
Why does the sea rush to shore?
Don't they know it's the end of the world
'Cause you don't love me any more

Why do the birds go on singing?
Why do the stars glow above?
Don't they know it's the end of the world
It ended when I lost your love

I wake up in the morning and I wonder
Why everything's the same as it was
I can't understand, no, I can't understand
How life goes on the way it does

Why does my heart go on beating?
Why do these eyes of mine cry?
Don't they know it's the end of the world
It ended when you said goodbye

Why does my heart go on beating?
Why do these eyes of mine cry?
Don't they know it's the end of the world
It ended when you said goodbye

When I am open, I am the party

When I am closed, I am not the party

Caribbean Mystery At The Museum Of Loneliness   III / XIV
Chris Petit *(presents an evening of his
re-forgotten film work)*

STANLEY SCHTINTER: The Liberated Film Club is running throughout July on Friday, Saturday and Sunday here at Close-Up. Nobody knows what's going on, including our guests. Tonight is a slight anomaly, as we have advertised an evening of films by Chris Petit. It's true: you are going to see films by Chris Petit. But regarding the rest of the season, trust no available information. These pamphlet descriptions are prompts for the unknown.

In celebration of this month, we have produced a Liberated Film *Cub*. It is a trans-USB pen with fashionable decapitation mode. On it there are four or ten films depending on the appetite of the cub. There are purge.xxx cassettes available too, including conversations with Derek Raymond and music with Mordant. You are here and so I take it you know Petit's work—but not what is on these tapes. And I'd be surprised if anyone knows the films we're showing tonight. By way of introduction... Petit has consistently refused to comply to the linearity, or the inertia that 'career' demands. He is the seer in the rear-view mirror; comets over the autobahn; the man at the other end of the bar, and he is you and I, waiting in the kitchen with a potato in each hand, knowing not what, why or how we got there. I am honoured to call him too my teacher. Healthy round of applause, please, Chris Petit!

CHRIS PETIT: When I was asked to put a programme together I couldn't think of anything to show. I thought about putting in some films that I hadn't actually directed and claim that I had directed them. The perfect answer to that was *Miss Marple: A Caribbean Mystery*, which I did direct as much as I was on the set when it was being filmed.

I thought that I was making my version of *I Walked with A Zombie*... 'Not with a BBC crew,' they said. I don't know why I was asked to direct *Marple*, but the reason I agreed in the end was Joan Hickson. I always liked her as an actress. And the *Marple* series? I didn't like the production values; I didn't like the vintage; I didn't like the camp quality, but for the fact that they had to export everything to the Caribbean for the exteriors, which meant I was able to get rid of the vintage cars, in fact all of it. My only note to the actors was *no camping it up*. The problem with Joan by then—she was 82—was that she had to be seated for you to get any lines out of her. So, all of my tracking shots went out of the window. We put Donald Pleasence in a wheelchair, so they were both the same height.

One morning, I thought *fuck it*: we're going for the tracking shot. She only had a short speech to make as she left the church. I think she had to start with saying 'A lonely life the Major's...' And that was as far as she got. We spent the whole morning trying to do this walking and talking sequence. I can't remember whether it's in the film or not, but maybe you'll spot it.

The only other thing I want to say tonight is a cautionary tale about English cinema. About a year ago, I had to do a thing at the Barbican which was the expected routine of 'what are *we*—English cinema—going to be like in 10 years? What's our wonderful vision going to be?' I rather spoilt the party by saying: 'Well, if you're going to look 10 years ahead, you have to also look 10 years back, and ask yourself how much has changed? The answer is not very much. In 10 years' time, you will still be watching Ken Loach films, so you better get used to it.' Anyway, connected to that was the fact that I really wanted to do one more film. Not the kind of experimental stuff you see at the beginning of tonight's programme, but a 'proper' feature film. I came across a book by the so-called 'queen of English noir.' It had two or three workable things in it: set in the 1980s; involved a few boisterous teenagers; had a nasty edge and two very unpleasant male characters. Schtinter and I fell in together over it because he was the only person I knew who would write it for such little money. And he fully embarked on this adventure.

The big problem, looking at the book, was that you have a story set over fifteen years involving the same characters. In the first part they're aged 15 and in the second part they're aged 30. So, what do you do? I mean, what do you do in terms of actors? Do you cast 22-year-olds, and say 'today you're 15, tomorrow you're 30'? Or do you take lookalike actors? It was a huge problem. There was no way of putting the two together, until Schtinter came up with a really brilliant solution, which I'm not going to share with you because you'll nick it. But it absolutely solved the problem, and in solving the problem it released the other half of the narrative form, to become something advanced and radically different from the standard English approach to... indeed *all* cinema.

The only brief I gave Schtinter was no swearing and set English cinema back by at least 35 years. He produced a fine, fine piece of work. There was really something there. And then the bloody 'writer' said *no*! She would not renew the rights to the novel. She hated it that much. So, it goes into a file which I've had for a long time, which is not just me, but this notion of all films that have never been made. Hitchcock's got them, Michael Powell had them, and out of this kind of Museum of Loneliness project is to, in a way, come up with a ghost-history of films that never got made. This one fits in without any effort at all because it's not going to get made...

ss: It will be made!

cp: We have to find other ways of making without making; we move fully into the age of post-cinema. Congratulations to you all for not doing Iceland vs. France. I'm very grateful. I would give *Marple* about forty minutes and then go home for the rest of the game.

Google mistakes when confronted by Liberated Film.
Think Murnau's Faust on holiday in Buñuel's Spain with
an Argentinean José Gaspar, a giant bouncy ball, and
the command internal eternal...

insert:

INTERRUPTION (1)

I dreamt last night of Andrea Luka Zimmerman. I dreamt of arbitrary lines drawn in sand. Decorating a side of the line formerly known as our sand lay familiar sachets of sugar. We had not noticed the lines before. It was Ella, the Staffordshire terrier, who bit first; and most sachets were found to be empty. The few that weren't became sand. It was Andrea's step that began the disappearance of the border and as we all walked, I turned and saw only footprints behind us. Thousands of footprints. There was a man too, the proprietor—I think—of the Mettle & Poise development on Hackney Road. As the distance grew, he froze, a render ghost: red hair, green coat, salmon and cream cheese bagel, and then the screen turned to static and then the power was pulled.

Ahead the sand is softer, we lose our shoes, indeed our clothes. I have with me only the photographs of that cafe in Paris, but I can't share them until I find a scanner. Ahead, there are trees, and to my side the sea. The sea looks different.

ANDREA LUKA ZIMMERMAN: I don't know if any of you have a dog? It doesn't matter if you don't.

Ella [In attendance; sat stage left] was a rescue dog, and she would've been put down.

I made a film about street dogs in Istanbul called *Taşkafa*, and I was working with John Berger on the issue of coexistence, asking: 'How does power work?' Not everyone will feel the full force of power, with their body, through their being, subjected to it.

The film for me was a way to explore how, where dogs are allowed to roam the streets in peaceful coexistence with the human population, they make their life, whereas here, in the UK we put them down and call it 'humanely.' While I made the film in Istanbul, dogs were in lecture theatres, courtyards, public squares, at the shore, at the foot of diners, and also, those that did not like to co-exist with humans in that way, lived in the forested hills.

We need unconventional ways to tell stories, and we need to ask the questions that aren't asked. History is not conventional. It is not straight-forward. My work is very often low budget to try to maintain the freedom my manifesto explores: freedom of the filmmaker, the person, and of co- existence. Its title is *Manifesto for Coexistence in Film and Life* (grand titles are a prerequisite of the medium). There are ten points which I'd like to read to you now...

1   Life is a work in process: unfinished, provisional and un-
    certain.

    Film must reflect this, or it has no purchase on reality.

2   A work seeking internationalist reception—through con-
    tent, form, aesthetic or technology—without a specific
    grounding in the lived experience of people and place, is
    not internationalist.

3   All filmmaking that is worth the name, regardless of its
    apparent construction, is a process of making *through* com-
    munity, on screen, behind the camera, and in the intention
    of all its makers. There is such a thing as society.

4   The budget and production structure of a film should
    always be in proportion and humane relationship to its
    protagonists, its theme, and its intention. It should
    be modest.

5   The most productive form of filmmaking today, regardless
    of its outward expression (fiction, documentary, *et cetera*)
    is the sketch, the essay, from the French, *essayer*, to try.

6   Heightened realism in filmic expression is both desired
    and the making manifest of what is latent in the material,
    waiting. Sometimes metaphors need to be expressed
    literally.

7   Braudel identified three strata in time—the personal, the
    social and the natural. The fourth dimension is empathy.
    Film is this fourth dimension, gently held.

8   All films must feature animals. Without them, it is like a
    camera without tape, without a reel. It ignores the majority
    world. It is not legitimate.

9   In the same way, a world—and a film—without hope, is
    invalid. Hope is the thing.

10

...the 10th is for you to decide.
        This is how things come together.
    Ella is rolling around.

In Communist Poland as in Capitalist Britain: climb the ladder,
lose your soul. But the journey was worth it, right?
Sneakers, trophy, finger, exit.

INTERRUPTION (2)

I dreamt last night of William Fowler, and William Fowler had a scanner. Archivist and tribesman, he resists the ships of the green disease on London today. Fowler is not afraid of the elevator, but Fowler won't take the hand. Fowler gets high. Fowler is flame retardant celluloid, avant-peacemaker dedicated to uncovering hidden cultural lineages; dedicated to height and ground zero but no floor in-between.

A record of this evening's passing was corrupted; in the absence of either aural or visual evidence, Fowler recalls his presentation as follows...

I'd been into Charlie Fox's writing for a while; I liked how, when discussing artist film, he described it in terms of feeling and what it evoked, sensually or sensorially. He didn't try to deconstruct films, but somehow still managed to do so by coming from a different direction. I later read something by him whereby he gave advice to would-be writers, saying you should try and expose yourself, make yourself vulnerable, take some kind of personal risk. It sounded dangerous and I liked it. I decided to reveal something about myself, taking Charlie Fox's advice quite literally. Though I didn't strip off. I told the audience that my dad had been sectioned when I was nine (for the second time, I later learnt) and he went from being a kind of god or hero to a monster. (It's one way to kill the policeman inside yourself, or a symbol of patriarchy). My mum told me he had been schizophrenic. I said all this. The people at Close-Up looked pretty nonplussed actually, and it was strangely anti-climactic but maybe it was a small personal victory. It would be tempting to rationalise this in light of how after my family fell in two, we effectively went into hiding from my dad and I was told not to tell people where we lived and the whole thing was a bit of a secret. This is all true by the way. Talking about it to a room of strangers at Close-Up thirty-odd years later should have been cathartic but it wasn't, at least not really. I think I was trying to shock myself. My mum and dad are both pretty long dead now; and all this history feels so long ago, almost like it happened to someone else, or to another part of my being. It had been an important part of my identity but was and is now largely out of reach. I filmed both myself and the audience with a Super 8 camera.

of the time
cinema with history and a future history
Greenaway
how it is made and what cinema is off the
screen
how it is financed and organised, and what
power is at stake.
But also what does it mean for us in the
room.
Binding us
Views.
communities   we make cinema.
A Team

Well, at last you get what you want:
you unrobe and face a door leading nowhere.

I had just been taken in an ambulance from Paris back to Norwich, after 10 days in intensive care at the Hôpital Cochin, Paris. I felt vulnerable and the world felt intimidating. So, although I really wanted to take up Stanley's invitation to introduce the films... I wasn't feeling up to it.

Several days later I woke up from a dream with a clear thought that I wanted to make some mayonnaise in the cinema before the screening.

No explanation, just a bit of magic; after all who would think that oil and raw egg could combine to make something so delicious.

There was no recipe—my mother taught me to make mayonnaise, not as 'cooking' but more like alchemy. There was always a jar in her fridge—often quite old with turquoise fuzzy stuff growing on the surface.

Use a whole egg—apparently no need to separate out the yolk.

Use an oil, like sunflower or grape seed, but not olive.

Mustard is important—it is the emulsifier—add a small teaspoon of Dijon.

Slowly pour in some oil while simultaneously whisking or blitzing or both.

The mixture will thicken.

Add some lemon juice or rice wine vinegar, salt, garlic.

And let the films begin.

The Faust of Murnau said no to baby-girl Buñuel and 'that' Spain. Alive and well he watches the fall of the wall from a television set in the South of France '...and it's our Europe what'll follow.'

COMMERCIAL—*The Third Worlder.*

NEXT—*The Third Planet.*

AFTER DINNER—*another kind of peace project... it's you and I and the empty garage.*

INTERRUPTION (3)

I dreamt last night of Ben Rivers. I dreamt that I couldn't find him. Rumours persisted of juice between the lid of the scanner and the surface bed, to which Sand whispered: 'If the glass of the document table gets dirty, clean it with a soft dry cloth.' Sand I had met at the correct time of night and in motion, curling together as question marks do in the backseat of a pool, until I stop, 'Stop!', alarmed by the possibility of erasing completely, rather than replicating, our writer and our river in the scan. Sand is reassuring as she falls out on to the pavement. 'Something we can do.' Her question mark unravels and re-ravels as an almost perfect circle. There is a vendor nearby with one thousand happy balloons and we buy them all. Next, I unravel myself and our two circles rise as a single figure 8, up above the city and out towards the trees. From this height the trees become just patterns and the city isn't and the river lost, winding through from sea to somewhere.

BEN RIVERS: I just asked Tony Grisoni—who is also going to introduce one of these events—'Why are we doing this?' Neither of us know (apart from for Gareth Evans, who was meant to be here tonight introducing me, but hasn't turned up). I did the same thing last week, when I was meant to be here to introduce *Days of Eclipse* by Aleksandr Sokurov, which happens to be my favourite film. The other reason I agreed was Close-Up: I applaud Damien and the team for everything they've done in their first year.

I was involved in something quite similar many years ago; it was exhausting. We did it for nine years and by the end of that I was ready to not do it anymore. I understand the amount of work that goes into this, and the love and the *complete* lack of money (which is probably worth mentioning).

I have no idea what this film is. In fact, I first asked Gareth for a date other than this one, because I really don't like Vincent Gallo. Gareth assured me: 'It's a red herring, don't worry. It can't be a Gallo movie. It can't be.' It can't be.

Buñuel is mentioned too in the synopsis for this event, and Buñuel I love. I read his name and thought immediately, 'Oh, I'll make some Martinis.' That was Buñuel's drink. But I'm not a cocktail maker and actually I prefer scotch. So everyone—me included—will have some scotch. Pass it around. It's relevant to what's up next.

This bottle... actually it was my birthday the other day and I...

DAMIEN SANVILLE: Oh, happy birthday!

BR: My dad sent me this. Shout if you haven't got one? This is how I often used to go about making films. When I would set out to make a film about somebody who's not so used to having a film made about them, I'd turn up with whisky just to get them onside, rather than to get them drunk. That's what I'm doing with you. Because I don't really know what to say.

DS: Can I have another one?

[Laughter]

Any doubles?

BR: She doesn't have one.

DS: More? It's delicious.

BR: Tony, have you got one?

TONY GRISONI: No, I haven't, I've been looking after everyone.

BR: Everyone is good?

AUDIENCE: Yeah. [Juddered harmony]

BR: It's Balvenie. It's good. There's a little left. Cheers.

AUDIENCE: Cheers. [General accord]

I want to read from one of my favourite books; *A Night of Serious Drinking* by René Daumal.

Daumal was French and Calais is mentioned in the synopsis and he's closely related to the Surrealists. It's a couple of pages, it might take five to ten minutes. The whole book is incredible. It's in three parts. In the first part the narrator is getting drunk with friends and enemies alike, then he moves into a paradise world where all of the people who can't drink any more are struggling to become supreme specialists in different subjects. While the narrator is going through this world, he keeps saying to himself '*I can't believe I went this long without having a drink...*'

[Professor Mumu speaks to our protagonist]

'I've grouped together the best Mancers of our time into an Institute where they work on a production line. The customer is examined there in turn by specialists in astral conjunction, tarots, lines on the hand, spots on the eyeball, intestinal noises, knucklebones, molten-lead shapes, dice, and the magic wand —in fact, in all the various means that Man uses in order to discover without covering or exposing, to understand without standing or sitting, or to become enlightened without lightening or darkening. And as all these people scrape together a living with thoughts like these: "*Me, I can* understand the secrets that free you from universal determinism... everything is subject to necessity, but *me, I can* participate in a superior reality... Man is overwhelmed by the shades of darkness, but *me, I can* partake of the secrets of the gods... *me, I can* comprehend... *me, I can*... *me, I can* do... *me, I can* exist in a transcendental state... .' We have consequently given them the generic name of the Meyie or Meyicans, and call their profession *Meyic*; these words they have taken over without understanding them, changing them slightly into *Magi*, *Magician*, and *Magic*. If you would care to follow me...'

'No thanks!' I said to him with a shudder. 'I have no wish to know anything which I have not worked hard to find out for myself. [...] In the process, I'd get left in a dustbin.'

'You are much too shrewd to be honest. But one thing you are still unaware of is that I have installed here an Abyssologist, as we called certified inspectors of dustbins. At least come along and see him at work.'*

*René Daumal, tr. D. Coward & E.A. Lovatt, *A Night of Serious Drinking* (Boulder, CO: Shambhala Publications, 1979), pp. 86–87.

JOHN ROGERS: I was only asked to do this yesterday and my first instinct was to say 'No.' I had planned a day of walking. But Gareth said: 'Do whatever you like! Last week someone made mayonnaise.' So, I cancelled my plans.

As a device to talk about Liberated Film: let's consider two cameras.

First, the Canon Zoom 814. A beautiful thing which I bought in Australia in 1997. I think it cost me fifty dollars which then was about twenty-five quid... now it's probably a grand.

I was at Sydney Film Festival when I got it, which was then largely held in the State Theatre: a beautiful 1920s picture palace. It has the second largest crystal chandelier in the world. The largest is in the Moscow Metro. At that time in the mid-90s, I was living with my wife—an actress—and everyone in Sydney was involved in some way in a short film. I mean everybody! It was more unusual to say that you weren't making a short film than that you were. I used to work at a building site and half of the guys there were making short films...

Anyway, I bought the camera in a hurry because the day before I'd seen Andrew Kötting's *Gallivant*, a visionary journey around the coast of Britain. Imagine *Coast*, the BBC TV show, but done by Hunter S. Thompson. That's pretty much *Gallivant*.

There's a great scene shot somewhere in Scotland: Andrew posts all of the yellow envelopes of Super 8 film to the laboratory, not knowing whether he'll get them back. The incredible jeopardy of that! You give everything to the film, you've got no idea what's on it, and you may never see it again. Something about that really captured my imagination.

I took the camera travelling through India. When I returned, I needed a projector and a screen to watch my footage. The bloke I bought them from in Brixton insisted on giving me a camera too, which was rubbish, so I gave it to my sister. She was about to start art school. She used the camera and went on to study an MA with (incidentally) Kötting as her tutor. A perfect symmetry.

In case you've never gone through the pain of this? There are three and a half minutes on a roll of Super 8 film. One film cost about fifteen quid, maybe eighteen quid now. That doesn't include the envelopes anymore and . . . a lot of the romance is gone, which is a disaster. You have to find someone to process it, and then to get it transferred digitally you're looking at another fifty quid. Most of the films I've made on here have been out of focus anyway. So, I stopped with this camera, but it was my first. I still love it.

This (gestures to second camera) is also a Canon. It's a point-and-shoot which I use to document my walks. Have you seen *Tornado* by Francis Alÿs? He runs into the eye of the storm. Stand on the street with this thing and you feel like that. It doesn't like the wind. But that aside, it works well: fits in the pocket, 16GB SD card... so I could probably get over an hour, maybe even two hours of footage. This to me is Liberated Film: you can make a film. We could do one now; my phone would be fine. We could upload it and people could watch it. When I bought this first camera that was unthinkable. But now, you could be on social media promoting it. You've got your production, your distribution and your marketing right there in your pocket...

There is a long lane at Pickett's Lock. Service roads for waste disposal. You have blokes in cars with fat arms. I went there today and thought, 'that's an ending.' This is an ending.

Spanish Civil War (MCMXXXVI–MMXVI)   IX/XIV
Gareth Evans

INTERRUPTION (4)

*I dreamt last night of Gareth Evans. I dreamt of the
great white barn owl launching from the walnut tree into
morning; I dreamt of the man who plants the seed and
who tends to the walnut tree; I dreamt of the man who
observes the tree; and the owl from it; the man beyond
the passer-by; I dreamt of the man who listens to the
interruption of the man at the next table; who gives time
to his dreams; his desires; their worth; of the man who,
by virtue of dashes in his little red book, forces the hand
of chance; of change.*

*I dream of the tree that makes the paper for the
pages of the book.*

I dream of the Islam that gave us paper.

*I dream of people driven from their homes, and
when I wake, I will not have to dream. I dream of the
siege of Paris in 1429, and then mix my numbers for the
mud huts of London in 1492, and then the Alhambra in
Granada at the same time, with kaleidoscope precision
and gardens, gardens. I dream of Christopher Columbus
going to sleep beneath a language he does not care to
know. I dream of him resting well and departing the next
morning, and killing, then, entire civilizations by touch
alone. I dream of peacock. Of nail varnish. Of avocado.
Of vascular disease. I dream, then, of education; of
school dinner inflation; of the pedagogic missions; the
second Spanish republic; the Megabus; the gay train;
Angela Eagle.*

*I dream of Federico García Lorca from a cave,
seeing all of the Sierra Nevada. I dream of him killed for
his language; for his somewhere, sometime, somehow.
I dream of sun curving and sky falling and calves born
backwards on grassless slopes. I dream of bloodied paper
dried by a pleading flame. I dream of Leonard Cohen
(and Leonard Cohen knows). I dream of Café Katie
approaching the walnut tree and crushing one underfoot.
I dream of the owl returning. I dream of feedback loops;
the coming cataclysm; and then the beginning again.
And I wake and I realise that I haven't been dreaming*

at all; but singing; singing the song that brother Gareth
gave me; somewhere, sometime, somehow.

[Singing now]

> *There's a place for us*
> *Somewhere a place for us*
> *Peace and quiet and open air*
> *Wait for us somewhere*
> *There's a time for us*
> *Someday there'll be a time for us*
> *Time together with time to spare*
> *Time to learn*
> *Time to care*
> *Someday*
> *Somewhere*
> *We'll find a new way of living*
> *We'll find there's a way of forgiving*
> *Somewhere...*

A NOTE TO THE READER—

> *The recording of this evening's introduction was spoiled;*
> *hence we have no transcript. Instead, an introduction to the*
> *introduction of another introduction, from one week prior.*

GARETH EVANS: Welcome back to those of you who have come to this esteemed venue before, and a huge welcome to those of you who are new to this wonderful arena of darkness, soon to be complete darkness of course, but then the light that comes from the screen will dazzle us all... This particular light will really dazzle us because it will be light that we guarantee none of you will ever have seen before, and if you have seen this particular gathering of light, then you can seriously come to the front of the house and demand all sorts of extra goodies—like, for example, a season pass for the rest of the Liberated Film Club month.

These are films that you will not be able to see anywhere else unless you have serious access to the darkest and weirdest corners of the global film archive. These are films of course gathered by Schtinter, a man who now only needs a surname.

To celebrate the first year of Close-Up as a cinema, a foundational stone is currently being hauled over to the Cereal Killer cafe (the location in which Close-Up was conceived as an idea and delivered as a library ten years ago). Extraordinary. It is now, of course, a cinema, a library, a cafe and bar, and it's basically an idea: an idea made brick or flesh.

I can see people in the back row yawning already, they've heard this before. I've used different words to say the same thing. I basically say the same thing each time. We're recording this so... tomorrow, or next time we're here, we'll just play that version?

Basically, it's a call to arms. It's a rallying to support this venue, which is very much in the scarcity leagues, in London but also in the UK as a whole. Not only is it founded and run by a French person—which of course is becoming a rarity, if not illegal in the coming future—it is supportive of cinemas and of film from Europe and across the world.

As Nicholas Parsons says on *Just a Minute* every week on Radio 4: 'We are delighted to welcome our guests from the UK and across the world.' We *are* delighted to welcome cinema, products, artefacts, titles and of course *audiences* from across the world to this wonderful venue. This month in particular is very special, as I said, because none of the films is known to the projectionist, to the front of house, and indeed to the founder of Close-Up... to myself or to the very special guests who introduce each screening. We have no idea what is going to be shown until it starts and whirls into action. That's a very particular thing. I can think of no other venue that I've ever encountered as an audience member, or as a kind of participant in the events, which would even *conceive* of doing that for one night. They would know between the lines and certain codes in place, that it will probably be a David Lynch film. Or maybe *2001*? *Et cetera, et cetera, et cetera.*

These codes are put into the signage here. The coding is deliberately designed to mislead and misalign you. This is a very interesting proposition, I think, and it's one that has been taken to about its natural limit over a month. That is what we are embarking on—thanks to Schtinter, who is in Paris, and who will shortly introduce **** ****** by video message. He is sending messages each night from Paris to the guest, specific to the guest. I will shortly let him begin, but before I do, I thought I should read a poem which sums that up very well. Much of this I don't understand, but I do like the last lines, so just bear with me. It's a little bit of a refrain, so if you learn it then feel free to say it with me. It's called 'The Waking' and it's by Theodor Roethke, a mid-century American poet too little valued.

'The Waking'*

I wake to sleep, and take my waking slow.
I feel my fate in what I cannot fear.
I learn by going where I have to go.

We think by feeling. What is there to know?
I hear my being dance from ear to ear.
I wake to sleep, and take my waking slow.

Of those so close beside me, which are you?
God bless the Ground! I shall walk softly there,
And learn by going where I have to go.

Light takes the Tree; but who can tell us how?
The lowly worm climbs up a winding stair;
I wake to sleep, and take my waking slow.

Great Nature has another thing to do
To you and me; so take the lively air,
And, lovely, learn by going where to go.

This shaking keeps me steady. I should know.
What falls away is always. And is near.
I wake to sleep and take my waking slow.
I learn by going where I have to go.

*Theodore Roethke, 'The Waking,' in *The Collected Poems of Theodore Roethke* (Doubleday, 1966), p.108.

To paraphrase Flaubert, and Buddha before him:
anything becomes connected depending on how you look
at it. A stranger lives in the house of another stranger.
The stranger can usually predict crimes. When a crime
doesn't happen, the universe is upset, and everyone
must pay.

A few words that I'd like to call 'IN PRAISE OF NOT KNOWING'.

So here we are: not knowing. Not knowing what it is that we are about to see. And I like not knowing. I like not knowing in general—a lot. Even when the film starts running up on that screen: that film will fill and hold my mind, knowing more about me than I know about it. It is tantalising. And it hasn't even started yet! Thé potential is wonderful! The film just now is next door, coiled up, tensed, waiting; holding what it knows. I'd like to say: thinking. And I am here waiting too, thinking that because it will start soon, in a moment, that somehow, I'm on top. All I have to do is wait. Then I'll know.

The observation of Marquis de Sade, that there is nothing as mysterious and beautiful as an unexplained scream heard emanating from a shuttered room in a high tower... at its best, cinema is like that for me. A mysterious scream—even when it's over. Worrying, humbling. And I like not naming absent things, even if I think of thought as an exhausting, endless naming of things. Cinema gives me a break from all that.

I like living at the limits of knowledge. I like not depending on or deferring to reputation. I like the idea that I might not need to look to precedent, or to canonical authority. The unexpected encounter, in half-light, my mind caught out, lagging behind—that's really something! It's not about a craving for novelty—it's about an elemental moment, a primal experience, about a challenge to everything we know and hang on to. It is vertiginous delight! (For that, thank you Schtinter!)

I like being at the limit of understanding, of knowledge, of exhaustive qualification. We believe the bridge we walk on will not collapse because stresses and strains have been calculated precisely; the structure is rigid, designed for utility and reliability. The rocket will reach Jupiter's orbit, precisely. And that's beautiful, because we trust in knowledge and expertise. We adore it. Yes, we do.

And yet, I recall the shock I felt when, as a student sitting in a lecture on the Foundations of Mathematics (Mathematics the beautiful pinnacle of human reason!): I heard about a thesis that announced that mathematics had at its heart a huge, insoluble problem. You may have heard of Kurt Gödel and the incompleteness theorem? His 1931 paper was a huge blow to people working to develop the perfect architecture of mathematics. It showed, incontrovertibly, that maths, or the truths that maths could express, might be unprovable. If the math was good enough to build bridges, it could not necessarily discover all of the truths it might express, or conversely that if it could prove all truths, it would also inevitably be able to prove a contradiction from which it would logically follow that the bridge would collapse. All deductions equally valid—even the false ones.

The thesis is an immense thing, but essentially what Gödel did was to provide a mapping of axioms and operators onto a field of numbers, and then use those numbers to provide statements about the maths. Thus, the fact that a theorem could be proved could now be expressed as a number, and for any 'Gödel number' arrived at in maths, there would be a bigger number that is itself a theorem about that number, itself needing further validation... *ad infinitum.*

'Beyond the best there is better' was the motto at my mother's school and sums up the problem pretty well.

The proof delights since it hinges on self-referential statements, such as 'this sentence is false'. Gödel had demonstrated a way that turned such self-referentiality into a sentence in maths, and so showed that consistent maths could not prove by strict deduction all of its truths.

It is a wonderful demonstration of reason leapfrogging a rule-bound world; of truth leapfrogging provability.

My mind raced wildly in that lecture hall to the thought that... that maybe truth is always like this? Requiring validation beyond the mere statement of a truth; references above and beyond the statement, beyond belief in the sufficient and exhaustive logical power of reason. We cannot simply depend on our systems of signification if we want to express all truths. And beauty, surely, is a kind of truth, so must be just like that too.

To go back to absent things, the things we don't know, things which can't be calculated and enumerated comprehensively—we confront the world of product, genre and category. For me the absent, unnamed things represent a challenge to that established order. The very idea that all truths, all we can experience and know, can be deduced from a few axiomatic assertions is surely an affront to the poetic possibility. And yet it is the prime and so very successful strategy of all established order.

We should (and must) resist, for—as the avant-garde project knew—we long deep down to travel beyond the communicable and make contact with the infinite potential of the mind, and so know more (if not everything), and learn to resist the suffocating and denying coils of the system that encloses us.

So...

NO to units of meaning!

NO to enumeration, list-making, star-rating!

NO to established opinion!

NO to control!

NO to expertise.

NO to introductions and commentary.

Instead...

YES, to reason that is full of light and infinite potential.

YES, to play, and the infinite.

YES, to cinema.

YES, to us here—and now.

On the closed door of the hardware store.
Argentinian pop singer to tackle teatime on screen.
Genet might have liked, Fassbinder too.

Genet never saw Fassbinder's adaptation of his Querelle, *as no cinema nearby was willing to host the extent of his cigarette smoking.*

INTERRUPTION (5)

*I dreamt last night of John Akomfrah. He carried a guitar,
and the song he played I had to hear again and again.
The song lifted me from the roundabout. From the tid-
dlywinks, from single screen projection. From the crying
game, and from the false promise of the craft brewery.*

*He spoke of fingerprints, sang of footprints, and
launched like the great owl into each morning. Peggy Lee
was there. So was Nicholas Ray. We had a cool time.*

*When John opened his mouth, everyone understood
that they too had mouths, and so everyone spoke. From
free voices came kisses, and the kisses became song.
The sound was not a muddle. It was not a competition.
It was clear, and everyone was heard.*

[Now singing]

*Play the guitar, play it again
My Johnny
Maybe you're cold but you're so warm inside
I was always a fool for my Johnny
For the one they call John Akomfrah*

JOHN AKOMFRAH: Here we are, upstaged by an unknown film and an unseen introduction, which was insanely complimentary, flattering, embarrassing. You know the gig: I really don't know what the film is, so I'm not sure how what I have to say will help. But it struck me that one possible thing I could do was remind you how in many ways the premise of this event, or these events, is in fact the premise of cinema. The impossible relation implied by the term itself is that you will be in anticipation, waiting for something to come, which despite all pretensions or claims to the contrary... will not come. That is the cinema. Even *Transformers* never quite delivers what it says on the tin. Our reception of cinema always remains transfigured, but it never really comes.

I started to think about how to connect this thought with what I think cinema has which is worth preserving: hope. Not 'hope' in the Obama-esque sense. The problem with that definition of hope is that it suggests you will come to hope and hope into being. We don't. We either, as Bloch says, 'commit to its arrival as the thing to come,' or not. It is a principle.

Three days ago, I went to introduce Andrei Tarkovsky's *Mirror*; I've seen this film just about more than any other film, and I thought 'I don't know what I'm going to see in it again.' But when it came on it was different. I saw and heard things that I hadn't before. It was unknown, and it is this transfiguration, this hope for the new image or sound which is bound to our relationship with cinema. The unknown event in particular perfectly mirrors what our relationship always is to the image.

I was led to think about which other films or people name this relation: and it's the central figure in *Close-Up* by Abbas Kiarostami that comes to mind. Hossein Sabzian. Every time he opens his mouth, in the film and afterwards, he says something about cinema which I think is worth holding onto. The last thing I read, in Kiarostami's obituary, was Sabzian saying: 'With every good film I see, I feel reborn.' Fucking deep, dude. And it seems to me that this question of rebirth is bound up with that one of hope which the cinema promises, because it effectively says that you will come into this room to watch Tarkovsky's *Mirror* (which you've seen sixty times), and you will leave with a new insight. This new insight will transform not just your former perceptions of the film, but of yourself. The image has that ability. It has the ability to remind you that it's both an attempt to register mortality—because of course every image you see dies the moment you've seen it—and a space, and one of the best we have, in which the opposite question of immortality is also wrestled with. It is this double motion of the image that cinema most invests in and most trusts.

I have no idea whether what I've said will help you navigate through this.

Good luck.

Meli, meli-num-num: the jobbing director from whom Genet stole and Warhol did too.

You've got a friend in me
You've got a friend in me
When the road looks rough ahead
And you're miles and miles from your nice warm bed
You just remember what your old pal said
Boy, you've got a friend in me
Yeah, you've got a friend in me
You've got a friend in me
You've got a friend in me
You got troubles, and I got 'em too
There isn't anything I wouldn't do for you
We stick together and we see it through
'Cause you've got a friend in me
You've got a friend in me
Some other folks might be a little bit smarter than I am
Bigger and stronger too, maybe
But none of them will ever love you the way I do
It's me and you, Shama

SHAMA KHANNA: On this coming Monday, it will be a month since Google disabled my blog and email account. They continue to offer not a single word of response to me or to anyone. This is what's new since my last update: some new, very kind people are reaching out to their contacts at Google trying to find out something, and I of course really hope something will come of this. I know that, thanks to the incredible amount of media attention, the petition, and your amazing public support, this situation has become a big crisis at Google. I'm told that the reason for their ongoing silence is because their legal department is trying to figure out a response that will paint them in the most positive light possible. One knowledgeable person I spoke to has speculated, not without logic, that I should prepare myself for the possibility that Google will respond in such a way as to paint me as the bad guy, possibly to the point of even launching legal proceedings against me. I can't imagine what basis there could possibly be to justify an action like that on their part, and no one really knows what's going on, but that's a disturbing idea, obviously. I guess Google will have to respond one way or another at some point, and I just hope it's very soon. That's it, for now. As ever and forever, thank you all so very much for supporting the blog and me in this crazy, inexplicable battle. Words fail, and I'm just deeply moved and so thankful to you. More news when there is more.

Dennis Cooper
Seven Poets Chosen by John Ashbery*

for Tim Dlugos

We are taking the obvious drugs.
We are stoning the oblivious adulterer.
We are sleeping with adults at last.
We are last in line for The Teardrop Explodes.
We are exploring vast nearby planets.
Our plants are wilting while we're on vacation.
We are vacating our new poems of meaning.
We are mean to the people we live with.
We are 'live' on talk radio.
We are living on top of radiation.
We radiate good health on the west coast.
We coast on poems we wrote eons ago.
We will never let Ian Young sleep with us.
We sleep where danger is least apparent.
We are parents to poets who write like us.
We are more right wing at the present.
We are less right wing than our President.
We write poems that sound like they're winging it.
It is quite interesting what we are doing.
We are the nice people cops are arresting.
We cop a few hours and think we look rested.
We are not what our horoscopes printed.
We have a Hockney print in our vicinity.
In this city, that's pretty hackneyed.
But if we could hack it, we'd buy a Winkfield.
We are the sickos beneath Tom Clark's hatchet.
Weld like to clock our time in his presence.
We are giving this present to beautiful people.
We are the dutiful people you see here.
We deal drugs at the foot of the suitable steeple.
We wear these suits for an obvious purpose.
We'll tote our purses into oblivion.
We purse our lips to indicate our totalitarianism.
We were totally flipped out on acid.

*See Various Artists, *English as a Second Language; Talking Package*
(Freeway Records, 1983); the preceding text on p.125 also owes to Cooper.

The source of our flippancy is chemical.
We slept in the doorway to the polemical.
We kneel on the floor near the collectible.
We place tape on the mouths of the kneeling.
We write a play-on-words rocketing outward.
We play good quality punk rock from England.
We were a rock, now we're an island.

Tiny Argonauts
(Beyond Lost & Beyond Love)
Tony Grisoni

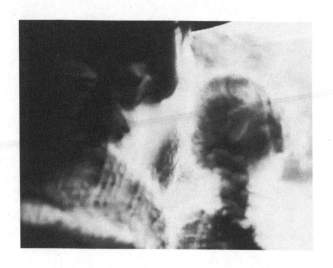

Deeper reading the heroes of old uncovers a fact thought lost to cinema: the adventures, achievements and amendments of our characters—e.g., Theseus— happened long before the age of consent (16 in the UK). From the director of the last and greatest melodrama (14 in Germany).

INTERRUPTION (6)

I dreamt last night of Tony Grisoni. I was living in a pipe at the time, or a piece at least; that same piece or so I believe, from the sand at Robin Hood's Bay, where mum and dad and I would lie in a one-man tent and talk about next year. From the tent or the pipe Grisoni fell and spoke about the flood. 'Come on board, man' and, with masking tape over each end of the pipe, the big wave took us sailing towards the big boat, Brooklyn, Syros. On board the big boat was an Australian. 'You don't know what you're missing,' it said, and then edging towards the tank, 'Kid, the name's Ruby, kid, I'm online, find me,' it jumped. The deck was slippery and Grisoni laughed and lunged at me with his tape but missed and the potato in my hand developed a mesh and became a potato microphone and, over the ship's tannoy, the captain's cue...

[Now singing]

Tony Grisoni
*I'm not just one of your little toys
Don't say I can't go with other boys*

*And don't tell me what to do
And don't tell me what to say
And don't, when I'm on deck with you
Don't put me on display*

TONY GRISONI: Ben Rivers played a very clever trick for his introduction: he had a bottle of scotch and he dished it out. We haven't scotch. We have hooch. Homemade, probably illegal. It's a good idea you all have some. Pass it around.

It's fine. It's pure. It's from my house. Rivers worked the scotch into his introduction. I'm not going to do that. I'm giving you hooch because I thought it'd be nice to have a drink.

I used to take any job that was offered to me. I got a dumb adaptation of a dumb book. It was about twin sisters. One sister got killed, and the other sister had to find out who killed her and why. I wrote the script and submitted the first draft. The producers called and said, 'this is meant to be a thriller.' And I said, 'Yes, but she's mourning the death of her sister.' Their response was, 'for fifteen pages?' And I said, 'Yeah—how long should she mourn for?!'

'Half a page maximum: she has to get on with finding out who killed her and why.'

In the novel there's a boyfriend, and every time he turns up as the cavalry, the saviour. I couldn't stand this, so I changed it: each time the boyfriend turned up he made things worse. Nobody seemed to notice. We shot the film. It was only when the producer saw the first cut that he said, 'The boyfriend. He's a real wimp.' And I confirmed that yes, he was, and it was a kind of joke. The producer didn't find it funny. He said that I had to make him stronger. My obvious response to this was: we've shot the film! It's impossible! But the producer assured me not to worry; that I should write something 'really strong' for the boyfriend, and when he turns his back to the camera, or off-screen, those lines would be overdubbed. I asked if they were sure. They were sure. A little time went by and I decided I had to walk away from the project.

I couldn't do it. But they did write some really 'strong' lines for him, and so in the film you have this wimpish boyfriend, but every time he turns away, he is really fucking insistent. It actually became a pretty amazing character.

But this sort of situation, which you usually find with executive producers in the mainstream is... a tricky one. It is a game, and it is just what you take on when you do this particular thing. I was very lucky. I got my first job in production from an extraordinary man, a producer called Tony Garnett. In 2009 he wrote an open letter sharing his professional experiences, most of which came from the BBC. It was titled: 'How to kill creativity while claiming to help it grow: A lesson in New Labour double-think.' And I recall that the first time I met him, he asked if I'd heard of the 'auteur theory.' I told him I had studied it at college, and he said 'Bollocks. It's vanity.' Anyway... I can't find it (the text). A pity because he writes so well, and a perfect segue into my willingness to do pretty much anything to avoid writing. Including this talk.

I've avoided writing in lots of ways, one I think worth mentioning is the excitement I've felt thinking about a cinema which existed before I experienced the cinema, in a very early, pre-verbal way. It is somehow wrapped up in the colour blue. Not the "Derek Jarman" Blue, but the night of Technicolor blue; the earliest I remember it is in Walt Disney's *Zorro*. A beautiful blue.

Here, lucky dip! Calotypes. I have lots of props. Another thing I use to not write. These are experiments—you, Miss, have one of the worst experiments—and then I thought: I won't write again about story or character or anything like that. I'll just write about blue. I got very excited about this and discovered woad. I found out how to make it and I dye things. I dyed this vest. Blue. These natural dyes rub off into your skin and I thought that people once used natural dyes as a kind of self-medication? That's what I'm doing: wearing my Technicolor blue. Wearing cinema, somehow.

Another way I have avoided writing is with Terry Gilliam. For *Fear & Loathing In Las Vegas*, we agreed that we wouldn't write anything because Hunter S. Thompson wrote so brilliantly. Why would you try and re-write him? Instead: collage.

The next amazing discovery—again un-writing—was with Michael Winterbottom on *In This World*. We had the idea of a film about two guys travelling overland from a camp for refugees in Pakistan, across Pakistan, across Afghanistan, across Turkey, and, eventually, arriving in London.

The idea was to use what 'film people' call 'real people' (which means non-professional actors) and shoot the film in a documentary fashion. To shoot as you go, as a road movie. It was fantastic and it robbed me of everything I thought I knew about screenwriting. You can't write dialogue for non-professional actors, because you can't structure the thing in any 'proper' way, so instead I learnt how to do some make-up. Some of these guys, whilst on the run, would press hot coins into themselves as a reminder of what they were doing and where they came from.

It was exciting too because I didn't make anything up. I met people and asked them to tell me their story. This was a difficult thing for them because they didn't know me and didn't know whether they could trust me. I looked a little like a policeman. Eventually, these people would tell me the details of these incredible journeys, and that formed everything that happened on *In This World*.

I noticed in the programme that this week is titled 'Beyond Lost & Beyond Love', and so—now I've found it—I would like to finish by reading a section from Tony Garnett's memoirs. I read the memoirs again recently, and I'm quite indebted to this man for giving me a job when nobody else would. He actively sought out people who weren't connected to film or TV in any way.

He was a very private man back then. You didn't know anything. He's now 80, and these memoirs are a lesson in reinvention. He has rediscovered and realigned himself, gone back, and back; he is a very brave man.

My own work went on under the radar. Few knew about it. It took over five years. The hardest work I've ever done, and the most painful. It is the work I'm most proud of. As with my career in films, I couldn't have got through it without help. When I look back, I see it as my life's work, and the only real accomplishment. Everything else is minor.

If Freud was right, there are people who cannot recover from their childhoods. People who don't know themselves. In my case it was a traumatic forgetting, and I devoted my life to not remembering. I'd spent years pretending on stage to be someone else, then further years telling stories on screen in order to excavate truths about other people.

[...]

I embarked on an autobiographical exploration, dreading what I might discover and the anguish it would evoke. It occurred to me if history is our way of concealing the past, what if my suspicions of my guilt, was a way of concealing my actual guilt?

What if this need to discover the hidden truth actually did reveal that, underneath, I was guilty of unimaginable crimes. Crimes that I couldn't fully imagine because I protectively repressed them. What could I discover; did I dare? It wasn't courage that finally drove me digging into my life. It was existential necessity.

[...]

High drama emerges the deeper you penetrate each individual's story. There is painful suffering, humour, courage, achievement and loss. Transcending all the petty resentments and bitterness felt here and there, what marks them all is love.

Love that sustains. Love that offers continuity. Love that gives life its meaning. Love that is renewed as each new generation takes its first unsteady steps under caring eyes.

I Can't Wait to Get Off Work and See My Baby
(and take him to Close-Up
to see an obscure Yugoslavian film)
Damien Sanville

Your husband and your son leave you?
Never wanted children anyway, and I don't recognise the man
walking away... so!
Escape into the infinite potential of your dreams, fantasies,
and necessarily distorted memories.

DAMIEN SANVILLE: My first idea to introduce this film was to read the letter Groucho Marx wrote to the Warner brothers. When Warner Brothers' legal department were notified of a forthcoming *Casablanca* spoof—*A Night in Casablanca*, featuring a character named 'Humphrey Bogus'—they requested more information about it from the Marx Brothers. Groucho, seeing the opportunity for a marketing coup, fabricated a lawsuit from the studio and wrote a humorous open letter about copyrighting names such as *Casablanca*, Warner or even Brothers, claiming Warner Bros. had strongly objected to the spoof's name.

Tonight, there might have been an FBI warning logo on the screen, and probably a short exposé on my part about copyright infringement and our responsibility to show these films regardless. As Godard once said, 'You do not have the right to show it, it is your duty.' But then I thought of something more in tune with the title of this last weekend of the Liberated Film Club.

Lights go out.
Room black.
Schubert's 'Piano Sonata in A major, D.959
(Second Movement)' plays in full.

NOW (MMXIX / MMXX)

An Old, Ochre Wall in Tuscany
(Shadows on the hills)
Mania Akbari

LADIES AND GENTLEMEN, welcome to the Liberated Film Club in its new monthly home in London's only cinema: Close-Up.

Usually falling at the end of each month, every single event will be free to members of Close-Up and cheap for any fool who isn't. Fucks or no fucks brothers and sisters, all y'all are in the building because you're sick of knowing exactly what you're going to get, and you're sick when you get it. Please welcome with a warm hand... first to the stage tonight: Mr. Mundo Breadcrumb!

MUNDO BREADCRUMB: Thank you very much everybody.

My name is Mundo Breadcrumb.

[Light laughter from the audience]

I have a quote from René Descartes: 'I think therefore I am.'

Designed by Traven T. Croves, a risograph print signed by Mania.

[BREADCRUMB digs in a plastic bag]

The fourth Liberated Film Catalogue, featuring lost, suppressed and impossible cinema: two pounds.

[Another round in the lucky dip]

The fifth Liberated Film Catalogue...

[BREADCRUMB grunts loudly, eliciting a little more laughter from the audience]

...a bloodied Gregg's wrapper: three pounds.

[BREADCRUMB digs in a little deeper]

Special edition with vegan sausage roll: thirty pounds.

I'm sorry Stanley can't be here tonight, but he will appear now via live video introduction.
Thank you.

[Laughter and applause]

INTERRUPTION (7)

I dreamt last night of Mania Akbari. Mania, in my dream,
defined civilisation as the afternoon light that falls on an
old, ochre wall in Tuscany, and asked me, 'When did you,
Stanley, last see such light?' I stopped to think, as I so
rarely do, and in my stopping saw it. The afternoon light
on the old, ochre wall in Tuscany was there in Mania. I
watched that light until night, and said to someone next
to me, 'The majesty of art, and its great burden: to share
the dream of all and master it. Yea, the reaper cometh.'
The person—I don't remember who—told me to calm
down. A call was made, and a holiday was declared, and
someone wrote a theme tune for it, for her, for Mania...

[A lone guitar accompanies a voice, singing]

Mania Akbari night
Paint your palette blue and grey
Look out on a summer's day
With eyes that know the darkness in my soul
Shadows on the hills
Sketch the trees and the daffodils
Catch the breeze and the winter chills
In colours on the snowy linen land

Now I understand
What you tried to say to me
And how you suffered for your sanity
And how you tried to set them free
They would not listen, they did not know how
I wonder if they'll listen now

Mania Akbari night, misty night
and the Liberated Film Club
        Listen...
Mania... Akbari...

MANIA AKBARI: A few years ago, I had an email from a friend:

Hi Dear,

*I remember that first time you took the Hafez book and
opened it and read.*

*I never did find out what that poem was about, but you said
it was a beautiful choice.*

*On the way home I thought about this tradition, and also
about a story from school. When I was young, I had to go to
church every morning. I remember one day a sermon in which
we were told to never do this, it seems it is not allowed in
Christianity. How strange I was maybe nine or ten years old
and I remember it so clearly. It told a story of a man looking
for a direction in his life. So, he decided to pick a passage
from the bible. I remember there were three lines he picked at
random. The first time he finds a line about Judas hanging
himself. He is not happy with this message, so he tries again,
the second passage says, 'go and do likewise,' again he is un-
happy, the third line says, 'what you have to do, do quickly.'*

*It was meant to teach us never to look for answers in
this way.*

I prefer your way

:)

Hafez was a Persian poet from Iran, and all people in Iran have
this book at home.

I opened it last night, for the audience, at random;
and now I'm reading...

گر از این منزل ویران به سوی خانه روم	دگر آنجا که روم عاقل و فرزانه روم

زین سفر گر به سلامت به وطن باز رسم	نذر کردم که هم از راه به میخانه روم

تا بگویم که چه کشفم شد از این سیر و سلوک	به در صومعه با بربط و پیمانه روم

آشنایان ره عشق در این بحر عمیق   غرقه گشتند و نگشتند به آب آلوده

بعد از این دست من و دامن آن سرو بلند   که به بالای چمان از بن و بیخم برکند

گر ببینم خم ابروی چو محرابش باز   سجده شکر کنم و از پی شکرانه روم

خرم آن دم که چو حافظ به تولای وزیر

سرخوش از میکده با دوست به کاشانه روم

When I head home from this abandoned abode
I will return there as a rational and learned man.

Should I return from this journey in safety to my homeland
I have vowed that I will go straight from the road to the tavern!

That I may recount what was revealed to me on this seeker's journey
To the monastery's door I will go with an oud and a goblet!

Should those familiar with the path of love seek to drink my very blood
I would be a wretch if I turned to the stranger in protest!

From here on it is but my hands and the chain-like locks of the beloved;
For how long should I seek the ways of the maddened heart?

If I see the curve of his mihrab-like brows once again
I will prostrate in praise and follow [the path of] gratitude!

Happy that moment when like Hafez—in the company of the vizier—
I will leave the tavern drunk with the beloved and head for home!

—Hafez, trans. Sahba Shayani, 'Ghazal 360'

Sylvia Plath
(Suicided for the Communist Cause)
Xiaolu Guo

LADIES, GENTLEMEN, NON-CONFORMULISTS;
and anyone related to Damien Sanville...

Welcome to the Liberated Film Club in its new monthly home
at London's only cinema, Close-Up. Usually falling at the end of
each month, every single event will be free for members of
Close-Up and cheap for any fool who isn't, provided you aren't
cannon fodder for a movie like a Mike Leigh OB-Eh?

[Cocks rifle]

Fucks or no fucks my people, all y'all are in the building, and
all y'all... because you're sick of knowing exactly what you're
going to get and you're sick when you get it.

Picturehouse!

[A bullet fired]

Curzon!

[A bullet fired]

Need I go on?
OK!

BFI!

[Bullets fired]

Remember the last time you went there with a promise of a
leap into the unknown only to find that the BFI holds as much
mystery as there is beauty in the people of Worcestershire?

Never forget.

So! Back by popular demand, a warm hand please for—first
to the stage tonight...
Mr. Mundo Breadcrumb!

[The theme music to ITV's *Emmerdale* plays in part]

Stop, stop... uh, apologies people. It seems that Mundo—like our, ah, our curator Stanley—cannot actually be with us tonight. I understand though that we have a replacement, yeah? Really? So, to introduce our special guest, please welcome—with a warm hand—first to the stage tonight, Mr. Stevie Wonder!

[Now singing]

No New Year's Day to celebrate
No chocolate covered candy hearts to give away
No first of spring
No song to sing
In fact here's just another ordinary day

No April rain
No flowers bloom
No wedding Saturday within the month of June
But what it is, is something true
Made up of these three words that I must say to you

I just called to say Xiaolu Guo
I just called to say how much I care
I just called to say Xiaolu Guo
And I mean it from the bottom of my heart

No summer's high
No warm July
No harvest moon to light one tender August night
No autumn breeze
No falling leaves
Not even time for birds to fly to southern skies

No Libra sun
No Halloween
No giving thanks to all the Christmas joy you bring
But what it is, though old so new
To fill your heart like no three words could ever do
I just called to say Xiaolu Guo
I just called to say how much I care, I do

I just called to say Xiaolu Guo
And I mean it from the bottom of my heart
I just called to say Xiaolu Guo
I just called to say how much I care, I do
I just called to say Xiaolu Guo
And I mean it from the bottom of my heart, of my heart,
Of my heart

XIAOLU GUO: I'm crying, but kind of genuine tears.

[The audience laughs]

Thank God there's a cinema like this left in London, really. You would imagine this only existing in the sixties, especially these days. It's impossible to survive.

So thank you, Stanley, for tonight.

And Damien—and Gareth—who'll come later from Whitechapel.

They didn't tell me what kind of a film that they're going to show, but I could vaguely sense that it would be something quite nice (at least, I hope). So, what should I talk about?

They said, *'feel free! just give us several minutes of your mind,'* but this Stevie Wonder thing has emptied mine…

[The audience laughs again]

I'd prepared some very, very serious stuff, but that pop song took away all of my intelligence.

It is beautiful seeing everyone here, though. It's really so tough for this kind of style to survive… I know that first-hand, as sometimes I'll enter some of my own screenings in some little arthouse, and there's an audience of two; in some cases, one of them will be the projectionist.

Anyway, since I've no notion of any of this evening's films —since I don't know what's going to happen after me—I thought I'd talk about something I know from my experience as a film-maker.

Some of you know me very well, but for those of you that don't, I'll give a very short and condensed forty-five year's worth of CV.

I grew up in South China—in a little village near Shanghai —but toward the edge of the country, towards Taiwan, on the East China Sea. I grew up without cinema or literature and, growing up in the early 70s, I was born at the end of the Cultural Revolution; I grew up in a completely pure, communistic environment. But by the end of the 70s, by the end of the Cultural Revolution, China had started to open up again and, by the mid-80s—when I was around eight years old—the government had begun to translate all your western stuff. So, we were starting to be able to understand when someone—a professor, say—mentioned an author like Balzac. 'Balzac...,' we'd say, 'I think he's some kind of painter?' Or 'Van Gogh, the American writer?' Information travelled slowly, but we—the younger generation—were extremely attracted to Western culture, and especially its intellectual output. So, whilst I'd grown up in this strange, extreme situation—a completely hygienic, North Korean style life and mindset—by the time I was around ten or twelve years old, a flood of western works was suddenly available. Because we were not in the WTO (which meant that commercial product was banned in China until, say, fifteen years ago) intellectual product was especially significant but required translation. We translated Duras, Jean Genet; Godard and Fassbinder; Pasolini's stuff.

Living in a little province, I began to write poetry. Stories. I didn't have any idea of cinema because, well, in a little province, in such circumstances... But it was there that I had my first encounter with censorship, and which I would like to say a few words about.

When you grow up in a situation like this, you do not know there is censorship. Like something from Orwell's *1984. What? What is censorship?* This is the life we have. There's no alternative. The first time I remember that something occurred in my brain, something sly and doubtful, I remember I was fourteen, fifteen. At that age, I was more attracted to ideas than I was anything physical, and I was reading a translation of Sylvia Plath. Her poetry.

In Chinese translations you would always have an editorial guide in the front and back of an edition, and often a very long preface written by the publisher's chief editor and, on the back, the cover would carry a blurb. I remember a Plath collection which said that this great woman had committed suicide because she hated the capitalistic system; she used her life *against* capitalism. For a young teenage girl from the provinces, this was powerful. Not because of the line about capitalism, but that she had killed herself. I was fascinated by this—I was of a very dangerous age—*how come somebody killed themselves?* Because my parents were both Communist Party members, it was an idea so alien to me... that a poet, an artist, wanted to kill herself.

Such vocabulary was forbidden in my life at that time.

I started to look for more stuff about suicide. You know, the typical thing a teenage poet would seek out. I discovered Plath's depression, but—in Chinese media—depression was always considered a product of society and, well, I still believe so as a Post-Marxist. I think any person's depression is a product of society; that there's no 'personal' in the world. I know I'm speaking in a society which believes in individuality, but I'm very doubtful of such concepts. But anyway, I discovered more stories about this poet, about Sylvia Plath, and I think that was my only direct encounter with censorship at that time: a vague idea of what should be told, *officially*, and what should not be told.

I left my hometown when I was twenty, and I went to film school in Beijing. There's a very good film school there, the Beijing Film Academy, which is where most of the filmmakers in China would go. I was already encountering continuous censorship in publishing houses as a young writer, and so (naïvely), I thought *Cinema!* A vivid and immediate media! You make images and the image speaks for itself! Maybe *there* there's no censorship? Or perhaps not so much as with printed matter, at least. You cannot print alone, of course—you have to go through a publisher—and I thought maybe the film world would be a less censored and monitored space. So, I went to film school, and that's where I stayed for seven years. In China a BA was four years, and an MA was three, so it was a *forever...* For all my youth, I'd ended up in school and, even there, I encountered a large degree of censorship. I remember the first film script I wrote that I felt was very strong (there's a kind of depression that accompanies my film career). My first long feature film. I mean, I don't mention my shorts, because we produced a lot as students, but this was the first long one I wrote: *Lovers in the Age of the Internet* (or *Lovers in the Internet Age*). It was a purely Chinese film, with certain silly remarks about the place of the internet in the early 1990s. We had the first-generation PC in China, I think in 1991, and I had one of these computers on which to write this script...

It was supposed to be my first feature film, co-collaborating with other graduates from the film school, but I recall the very damning censorship notes from China Film Bureau. Starting out, you'd have this huge body censoring your script way before you'd started filming. Even after you'd film, you then have to send off your footage; you develop your film (35mm at that time) only to see some of that footage censored; and only *then* you can you begin your edit, only to have that first draft censored as a cinedraft. It was a completely impossible journey to finish a film.

I was stuck at the first stage of this process.

The script was very simple: two lovers on a decade-long journey from student to Master of Film; on their way to becoming real adults; trying to find work, a job, a life... It's a *coming of age from school to society* story. The lovers live a young person's life in China—and I remember I received a note. Typed. Something like ten pages. I wrote about this in one of my books, *Once Upon a Time in the East* (a memoir published a few years ago)—and the complete note is reproduced there—but tonight, I'll cite another of the notes from the censorship of this script:

FROM MINUTE TEN ONWARD,
WE SUDDENLY SEE THE YOUNG LOVERS ASLEEP
ON THE SAME BED.
DO THEY MARRY?

IF YOU DO NOT HOLD A MARRIAGE
YOU HAVE TO CUT OUT THAT SCENE.

I thought—*Oh, I can't deal with that!*—so, we added a scene; a single sentence—

CAMERA PANS ALONG THE WALL,
AND ABOVE THE BED IS A WEDDING PHOTOGRAPH;
PAN DOWN; TWO YOUNG LOVERS, KISSING.

So, well, good, I thought: a cheap way to solve the problem without making this wedding happen. But the notes just went on forever, and it became more and more impossible to change the script any further.

Another I remember: the young lovers live in a hutong house. If you've been to Beijing, you know that a hutong house is subject to a kind of national pride. It's like a Victorian house here in England. Even though they're very old, cold, run down —and the toilets never work—it's the pride of it; some kind of architectural beauty that's the result of, well, some kind of historical value. A hutong is the same kind of thing. Obviously, indicative of a lower quality of life, but there's a certain kind of ecstatic reverie; the memory of China's imperial past (you know, I don't see the point); but anyway, in every hutong house there's never a working toilet, never a running tap, so you have to go out—leave the house and find another way to see to basic hygiene stuff. This young couple live in a hutong, they keep complaining about their hygiene, and so in came the note...

> THE HUTONG IS A GREAT ARCHITECTURAL
> ACHIEVEMENT IN ASIA AND CHINA;
> YOU MUST CHANGE THE CHARACTER'S TONE;
> CHANGE THIS ACTIVE CRITICISM OF THE HUTONG.

I was thinking about this, about the unknowns.

I was twenty-something, and that's really difficult to affect. Of course, technically, I can just delete all the complaints exchanged between these young lovers, but then their spirit would change; their love... This was a film about their (eventual) separation—and their divorce in end—so it would wholly change the story.

The note goes on:

> THE MOST IMPOSSIBLE TENET OF YOUR SCRIPT
> IS ITS NEGATIVE TONE;
> THE IMPOSSIBILITY OF YOUTH;
> THIS IS EXTREMELY GREY IN YOUR SCRIPT

huīsè (灰色): In Chinese, we say *huīsè de xīnqíng* (灰色的心情). That is to say, the script has this grey and painted kind of a mood...

So that was basically my encounter with censorship, and by the time we managed to make the film, I think I was basically on the verge of leaving China, so that's where we are.

I came here—to East London—and discovered liberation.

Thank you for bearing with me.

I hope the film will be great.

Whistler in 1885
(Shadows on the hills II)
Sean Price Williams

I'm not that busy; I barely put on clothes usually; I'm not a very active person. Uh, I was asked to do this... I introduced a movie that I really love once, one that I had nothing to do with, and I fumbled so badly, got very caught up in my own self-deprecation, and I ended up just destroying the movie I was introducing. Well, okay, but I don't even know what this movie is? It might be a movie that I don't even like, except... maybe... maybe it's something I'm interested in actually, so...

Anyway, I didn't know how to introduce it, and I don't want to say so much.

I'm here working in London. I live in New York. I'm a displaced American working here, and it's been an interesting time. I don't know. I haven't entirely connected with or figured out London yet, so I was looking at the other Americans that have lived in London. People that made the most of it and ended up living here for the rest of their lives. Today, we lost one of our great Americans in London: Scott Walker. He's been one of my guiding lights since I discovered anything that matters to me as an adult. So, I was pretty screwed up; working today, I couldn't really get my head around anything else. He was somebody that I had this weird fantasy of maybe meeting here in London, even though he's a notorious recluse. So, I kind of just wanted to play a few songs of his? And that's, kind of, you know, not that creative but... I don't want to sit in a light room with the light on me and listen to the songs, so I don't know how the best way of... I just want to hear a few of his songs that I picked. I don't know. That's what I wanted to do for an introduction to a movie and I don't know what it is. So... if I could do that? If we could just play these songs? And that's it.

Get another drink.

Get whatever else you need before this not-4-hour-movie.

I don't know.

Lights out
Music plays on...
Three songs...

'Nite Flights' /
'I Don't Want to Hear it Anymore' /
& 'Orpheus'

My plan originally was to read as much of Whistler's 10 O'Clock Lecture until someone fell asleep: an hour-long piece he delivered to people in Piccadilly in 1885. Super relevant. And it was, y'know, all about the state of art and warning people about the state of art... what's happening with art. I felt that it is relevant, between the lines again, and I really am feeling disconnected to what movie people are getting excited about and finding myself more and more and more exiled from conversation—when people get enthusiastic about Roma, for example, I don't know what to do; I can't help myself, so...

Anyway, there're these bad boys who've moved here —and Whistler was up there with the best of them.

SPW

The people have been harassed with Art in every guise—and vexed with many methods, as to its endurance—They have been told how they shall love Art! and live with it—Their homes have been invaded—their walls covered with paper—their very dress taken to task,—until roused at last, bewildered and filled with the doubts and discomforts of senseless suggestion, they resent such intrusion, and cast forth the false prophets, who have brought the very name of the beautiful into disrepute—and derision upon themselves—Alas! ladies and gentlemen—Art has been maligned—she has nought in common with such practices—She is a goddess of dainty thought—reticent of habit—abjuring all obtrusiveness—proposing in no way to better others—

She is withal selfishly occupied with her own perfection only—having no desire to teach—seeking and finding the beautiful in all conditions, and in all times—As did her high priest Rembrandt, when he saw picturesque grandeur and noble dignity in the Jews' quarter of Amsterdam—and lamented not that its inhabitants were not Greeks—As did Tintoret and Paul Veronese, among the Venetians—while not halting to change the brocaded silks for the classic draperies of Athens—

As did, at the Court of Philip, Velasquez, whose Infantas clad in inaesthetic hoops, are, as works of Art, of the same quality as the Elgin marbles—

No reformers were these great men—no improvers of the ways of others!—Their productions, alone, were their occupation, and, filled with the poetry of their science, they required not to alter their surroundings—for as the laws of their Art were revealed to them, they saw, in the development of their work, that real beauty, which, to them, was as much a matter of certainty and triumph, as is to the astronomer, the verification of the result, foreseen, with the light given to him alone—In all this, their world was completely severed from that of their fellow creatures, with whom, sentiment is mistaken for poetry, and for whom, there is no perfect work, that shall not be explained by the benefit conferred upon themselves—Humanity takes the place of Art—and God's creations are excused by their usefulness—Beauty is confounded with Virtue, and, before a work of Art, it is asked: 'What good shall it do?'

ATHINA TSANGARI: It's strange to have to introduce something you haven't seen. But in a way it's very similar to the process... to the moment where you are about to want to do something, and you don't know what that is, and you are on the verge of something, and it's very exciting and painful and embarrassing and humiliating, but at the same time a beautiful moment because of all of these reasons. And you have no idea. You just stand there. Usually what I do at that point is I throw the *I Ching*, and then, based on what the *I Ching* tells me, I just start writing; or, I choose the film that I'm going to watch at the moment; or, I choose what phone call I'm going to make; or what route I'm going to take on my bicycle; or what kind of fight I am going to have; or what kind of food I am going to cook; or what kind of case I'm going to give. So, I was editing today. It was quite painful and humiliating and embarrassing and exciting. And I was very nervous about doing this, so I did my charts. It directed me to this page, which I am going to read to you. Which is my introduction to the film you are going to see. And the page... Oh my god, I hope I can read it... And I am pretty sure that this is exactly the film you're about to see. So, it's 18, and it's *disruption*.

Disruption leads to great success. It is worthwhile to cross great rivers—three days before, or three days after. In disruption, there is hardness above and softness below. A flow of wind being stopped and disrupted. When disruption leads to great success, the world is pacified. It is beneficial to cross great rivers, in the sense that there is purpose in your actions. Three days before and three days after, refer to creative action, which begins again after it finishes—three days before or three days after. The image for this: there is wind under mountain —disruptive. Cultured people inspire others to develop virtue.

Night; desert; a man stands on its highway, lights a
cigarette; free hand elevated, thumb up for oncoming
traffic; a bus slows, turns; services; driver off, travellers
too; the man runs towards the bus; drops the cigarette;
climbs into the driver's street; picks up the microphone;
and sings...

Chloe, as free as the wind blows
As free as the grass grows
Chloe, to follow your heart
Chloe, and beauty surrounds you
The world still astounds you
Each time you look at a star
Stay free, where no walls divide you
You're free as the roaring tide
So there's no need to hide
Chloe, and life is worth living
But only worth living
'Cause you're Chloe

I

It all started with a miniscule green flare in the sky that after
wandering the universe and finding no corner in which to dwell
collected enough star dust to grow into a tiny comet which
then landed in Earth's ocean and after a few days, nourished by
salt water, exploded into tiny particles and each of these particles grew a webbed foot, and then several more, followed by a
rubbery body and a pair of round eyes. And the ocean, sensing a
new presence of life and happy to finally have company, adjusted
its temperature to make itself more welcoming.

The Reign of the Axolotl, ancient salamanders—amphibians native to the canals of Xochimilco in Mexico City—begins. Axolotls are able to regrow severed limbs and retain their infant features throughout their lives, never undergoing metamorphosis; therefore, all appear to be the same age and there is no hierarchy within their society. They are peaceful but lack assertive personalities, and as the world expands and more species come into existence, the axolotls are eventually replaced by the Feathered Serpent Quetzalcóatl, God of Wind and Wisdom, who reigns harmoniously.

III

A solar eclipse unbalances the cosmological order, Quetzalcóatl is dethroned, and a kingdom of shadows is established. This long night leads to the Reign of Quetzalcóatl's brother Tezcatlipoca, Smoking Mirror. Rivalry grows among the Aztec gods until they hand over earthly matters to man: Moctezuma is made emperor. The Spaniards arrive by sea, Moctezuma taken prisoner in his own palace. He is visited by Huitzilopochtli, god of war, as a hummingbird, who tells him the invading men are not gods and gives him a secret weapon. A bloody battle ensues. Defying all expectations, the Aztecs prevail, and the Spaniards are defeated.

In an obsidian mirror in Moctezuma's palace, an Aztec priestess glimpses scenes from past centuries elsewhere in the world. In ancient Greece, people gather in a planetarium and dream of reaching the stars. Enormous water-powered machines in the shape of dragons are installed on rivers in Tang Dynasty China. Somewhere on the Indian subcontinent, a species of macaque establishes control over all the temples but continues the practice of Buddhism. Women and children build two visions of paradise on earth: Petra, and Palmyra. Hundreds of thousands of migrating humpback whales sing and breach.

V

A mysterious epidemic has toppled the Roman Empire, felling its highest officials. Mass poisoning is suspected. In the Middle Ages, a disastrous plague, spread by giant spiders, sweeps the European continent. The spiders are finally wiped out by resilient cats brought over from Egypt. Tamed gargoyles help to erect grand cathedrals while monasteries fill up with anatomists of melancholy and the convents with female scribes. A new type of candle is invented that burns for fifty-five hours, leading to widespread insomnia. Herds of elephants and prides of lions roam the African continent, crowding out the human population.

VI

The Aztecs set sail for Europe on the Spanish boats that weren't
burned by Cortés, manned by conquistador slaves. The ships
land at Palos de la Frontera and a war of religion ensues. The
Virgin Mary is supplanted by Our Mother Tonantzin, maize
replaces wheat as a staple, cocoa beans become the most valued
currency. Madrid is the Aztec capital in Spain, but the human
sacrifice required to honour and appease the gods is carried out
at the Alhambra in Granada. The Aztecs are unable to extend
their influence further into Europe as they can't make it across
the Pyrenees.

VII

An enormous meteorite falls into the Zone of Silence, a mysterious part of the Mexican desert. All the principal Aztec priests
travel to visit the crater; as they stand inspecting it, another
huge meteorite falls and crushes them. The populace is freed,
no more human sacrifice. Under the mantle of black dust that
now enshrouds the country, the Spanish slaves revolt and spread
Christianity. Meanwhile, Berber hordes paddle across the Strait
of Gibraltar and wrest Spain from the Aztecs. Everywhere people
are reading the newly invented printed books. An unknown
breed of sea monster is spotted in the Pacific Ocean.

In Renaissance Italy, an artist draws a perfect circle while
pigeons invade the town squares before moving on to Constan-
tinople. Wooden flying machines are tried out, unsuccessfully,
from rooftops, causing dozens of deaths. In Germany, Jesuit
scholar Athanasius Kircher unsettles his fellow believers by cast-
ing demons on the wall with the help of a magic lantern. And
thanks to Galileo and his telescope, mountains are discovered
on the moon, unleashing a craze in the study of lunar topogra-
phy. Astronomers are astonished to find that the moon is in fact
the head of the dismembered Mexican goddess, Coyolxauhqui.

After a violent storm a series of dams bursts in seventeenth-century Holland, submerging its affluence under massive floods; entire communities migrate to the upper stories of windmills, and the country's most famous optics laboratory is inundated. From the small population of Sephardic Jews is born a new language, Hebrish, a combination of Hebrew and Flemish. Magnitude 9 earthquakes along the entire Eastern Pacific trigger a gigantic tsunami; the sea recoils and rushes back, devouring all life and construction in its path. In Britain, King Charles I and his army prevail, Oliver Cromwell is beheaded and there is rejoicing in Ireland.

X

In Russia Catherine the Great builds her Amber Room; two
wolfhounds from the palace get trapped in the amber and until
they are freed the country is declared in a state of emergency.
Much of Europe is overtaken by carnivals; masked orgies and incessant feasting fuel fantasies of inverting the established order.
Spanish botanist José Celestino Mutis's widely circulated book
about the dreams of plants triggers a small epidemic of mental
disturbances. Alexander von Humboldt visits Mexico and after
becoming attached to the volcano Iztaccihuatl, 'White Woman'
in Nahuatl, decides to reside permanently on her slopes.

On the eastern coast of the thirteen British colonies, American patriots revolt against foreign rule. During the Boston Tea Party, an entire shipment of chests of tea is dumped into the harbour, creating new breeds of overcaffeinated, electrified fish that rapidly grow in size and leap out of the water to bite British soldiers, drawn to the red of their uniforms. Iroquois, Algonquian, Wampanoag, Powhatan, Lenni-Lenape and other Indian tribes fight alongside the Patriots and independence is won. Tribal delegates take part in the Continental Congress.

In France it is the era of the air balloon, or *montgolfière*, enthusiasts: Louis VI sets his sights on the sky, hoping to expand his kingdom. All ascents are cut short by the French Revolution. The sans-culottes attack statues: to their surprise, certain statues fight back. The female knitters seated at the foot of the guillotine are found to be knitting back to life the cats killed in the 1730s cat massacre. Marie Antoinette escapes execution but is to be kept as a permanent exhibit in the former tiger enclosure at the Jardin des Plantes.

XIII

War breaks out between China and Japan over contested territory as well as claims to a rare species of dark blue nightingale said to summer in China and winter in the forests of Japan; for both countries, it is a national symbol. The war rages on for nearly two decades. After a year of deadlock, both sides back down and once they do, they realise that as a result of all the warfare, the fragile nightingale has gone extinct. Learning of the tragic loss, Maya in Mexico send flocks of resplendent quetzals to both countries.

The Industrial Revolution spreads across Europe. Thanks to the telegraph, occasional signals are picked up of ancient gods sending messages, but no one can interpret them. Women no longer work at the loom but receive equal wages to men in textile mills. An entrepreneurial Italian designs a tall, commanding puppet. For a brief time, this gives way to the Reign of Puppets. They supervise factories, drive steam engines, develop an obsession with cotton. The puppets are known to mistreat the children working for them. In a small town in Germany these conditions lead to the Children's Rebellion.

XV

Dozens of broad boulevards are laid out in nineteenth-century Paris during the renovation of the city. Congeries of spectres are released when the grounds are dug up and certain buildings demolished; the population more than triples. In Victorian England, mediums hold cabinet positions in the government and important matters are decided by tabletop conversations with spirits. Hurricane-force winds batter Patagonia, carrying thousands of feathers from Antarctic penguins to southernmost Chile and Argentina. Hieroglyphs on the Rosetta Stone are deciphered, yielding an account of attacks by Nile hippopotami and remedies for hippo bites.

Napoleon III sends Maximilian of Austria to become Emperor of Mexico. During a visit to the Yucatan, which is suffering a drought, Maximilian is pushed into the cenote at Chichen Itza to appease the Mayan rain god Chaac. Empress Carlota assumes his place, but grief drives her to madness; among her many follies, she endeavours to recreate Miramare, their castle in Trieste, on the coast of Veracruz. After a year she is deposed by Freemasons and ransomed by her brother Leopold II of Belgium. She spends her days in Bouchout Castle, holding long conversations with her pet armadillo.

After a 35-year-long dictatorship, Porfirio Diaz is ousted from power and immured in the Cananea copper mine; Francisco Madero seizes the presidency, setting off the Mexican Revolution. Revolutionaries across the land are assisted by armies of feral dogs, descendants of mastiffs and wolfhounds brought to the New World by Spanish conquistadors to attack and devour Indians, that have banded together to help overthrow feudal rule. A battalion of young girls under twelve-year-old Lupita Pérez joins Emiliano Zapata and victory follows victory. Lupita saves Zapata from an assassin's bullet and he becomes president. He distributes all the haciendas to landless peasants.

Sailors on the battleship Potemkin fight their way past Cossacks to Czar Nicholas II's palace and force feed the royal family rotten fish. The Romanovs are imprisoned, but rescued by a rain of wolves that descends moments before their planned execution. The family is granted asylum in Mexico, and sails before the revolutionaries can change their minds. Following Rasputin's murder, fortune-tellers exert their power over villages and 12 years of fighting ensue. Stalin dies leading the failed Kerensky Offensive, and with Lenin's support, Trotsky becomes head of Soviet Russia.

IXX

The Austro-Hungarian Empire has crumbled. Skies are permanently overcast, and a group of former ministers is seen in a field doing the Dance of Death. Among the 12 states carved out of the defunct Empire is Sintirom, a homeland where Romani people can wander at will. Rabid speculation in cocoa bean futures precipitates a worldwide stock market crash and a return to gold as the principal currency. Radio listeners in Spain, Italy and Germany are hypnotized by the voices of fascist dictators. Yeti yak herders are spotted in the Himalayas while a Sasquatch tribe migrates north to the Arctic tundra.

XX

In the early 1940s mass extermination of Jews is averted just in time by the appearance of the Golem. The towering clay figure makes a dramatic return, resurrected by Jewish mystics in order to save their people. He appears in Prague, and after single-handedly vanquishing Nazi troops at the border he marches into Germany, smashing fascists with his fists. Once his people are out of danger, and their dignity reinstated, he collapses into the mud, vanishing without a trace.

At the height of the Cold War, an unprecedented number of
birds is registered in both halves of Berlin, due to a high demand for passenger pigeons. A spy at the Sugar Research Foundation releases a secret study about sugar's role in heart disease;
sugar is banned in the United States, Cuba falls to Fidel Castro.
The United States and the USSR argue over the laws of outer
space—the legal status of cosmonauts, canines and launched
objects—but these remain too abstract to enforce. Mao Zedong
drowns while swimming in the Yangtse River, after colliding
with a baiji.

XXII

Humankind finally recognizes that animals have figured at every stage of human history. Unprecedented concern for animal welfare overspreads the globe. Poachers are imprisoned throughout Africa. A new generation of doctors in China debunks the myths of traditional Chinese medicine, slashing the demand for tiger parts, sea horses, totoaba swim bladders and rhinoceros' horns. Factory farming is banned, and slaughterhouses are slowly phased out in Europe and the United States—battles are still being fought elsewhere. The Japanese government shuts down the dolphin drive hunt at Taiji and outlaws whaling. The United Nations issues a 10-year moratorium on ocean fishing.

In Russia a famous troupe of clowns has taken control of the government. All circus bears are released but asked to report back should their advice be needed. Trade tensions erupt with Poland and Hungary over a new export tax on pickles and dessert wines. The country's two most accomplished female mathematicians defect during a world tournament in Iceland. Relations with the rest of the world depend on the outcome of an ongoing game of chess.

Along the US / Mexican border, gangs of narcosatanists are dismembering young women. The murders, shrouded in mystery, have been impossible to stop—until a female army of Tzitzimimes intervenes, with the help of migratory jaguars. The Tzitzimimes, or monsters of twilight, is also the name of an all-girl rock band that has mesmerized Mexico. Meanwhile, the axolotls in Xochimilco continue to worship their ancient deity, the Supreme Axolotl, knowing that all history is circular; they sense a coming cosmic crisis and are hatching a plan, growing new limbs and preparing for a novel planetary order. The world turns on its axis.

JULIET JACQUES: I've brought along this video case. For those who can't see, that's Vladimir Ilyich Lenin on the front. This is a Eureka Video boxset from 2002 called *Russia in Revolt*. It has three Sergei Eisenstein films in it—three of the early ones—and an Esfir Shub documentary, *The Fall of the Romanov Dynasty*. It's got Nicholas II on the back. I've been thinking about him this week because, on Twitter, I discovered a poem that I hadn't seen before by one of my favourite writers, the great Soviet poet, playwright, and filmmaker Vladimir Mayakovsky. It's called 'Eat Your Pineapple.' It simply says...

> *Eat your pineapple*
> *chew your grouse*
> *your last day dawns*
> *you bourgeois louse*

I was always told to learn poetry by heart, and I'm going to be carrying that one with me everywhere I go.

[Juliet played a game; the rules of the game
are outlined below]

I spent pretty much all of my student loan on stuff like this video.
I actually owe more money now than when I graduated in 2003.
I recently broke the five-figure mark with the interest. I now owe
the government £10,000. So, I will send this back to them, if
they ask for it back. I assume it's accumulated in value by now.
I think it's quite rare.
    I don't actually have the videos in here. They're at home.
Because what I've done is, when I graduated with ten grand
worth of debt (thanks Tony) I decided that the best way to clear
the debt would be to write for experimental film magazines.
I started writing for *Filmwaves* and, since then, I've written for
Vertigo, Cineaste, Sight & Sound, and I'm now a billionaire.
    Bourgeois louse...
    So, what I've done, because I didn't know what this film
was going to be, and didn't know how to do an intro that would
be appropriate to the film, is I've printed out and cut out... I've
been reading a lot of surrealist poetry lately, and there are these
sorts of exquisite-corpse-kind-of -games, cut-ups and whatnot.
I've cut out 40 short passages from film reviews I've written
over the years.
    You'll be delighted that this is an audience participation
night. I'm going to take this around the room, I'll pass it around.
Everyone is going to take one of the scraps of paper in this video
box. When everyone has a slip of paper, we're going to go around
the room and everyone's going to read out the sentence. We'll go
from the front this way along, second row, third row, fourth row.
What we will get, hopefully, is a sort of collective introduction
that will announce a kind of impossible film.

[This impossible film is detailed overleaf]

The latest and junkiest outing from the travelling opportunist
of gay cinema, this film is as much calculated to upset a heterosexual audience as to flatter the complicity of a male gay one.
Four days earlier, *The Observer*'s brief synopsis was equally scathing, but came closer to accurately describing its ensemble cast,
realizing that this was not, or at least not primarily, a gay film.
They described it as a transvestite / transsexual cabaret; one
which looks disparagingly like an amateur not on an off day.
There are some genuinely bizarre touches. The green alien, with
whom the child Wittgenstein discussed doubt and the existence
of martians, for example, playfully undercuts the film's self-as-
sured intelligence. The film opens with seven possible endings.
A woman tentatively opens a door, walking into a world of
film, and a farcical narrative where a fight between a man and
a woman is soon overtaken by footage of a robot—doubtless
intended to be frightening at the time, but preposterous
now—terrifies hiding residents of the house it destroys. When
the BBC produced this film, it's restrained [and] subversive use
of the documentary format pioneered during the 1930s (and
which would become televisual convention) show the effects of
a nuclear bomb hitting Rochester, [the film] was banned, [and]
More than a modernist movie—shot at night in Waterloo Station
and Lots Road Power Station (as well as Chelsea and Thistle
Grove Alley, and possibly Selfridges)—this film was about
London life and its parks, its department stores, and bedsits,
and how the tube, radio, and telephones had changed the urban
world. It focused on four ordinary, workaday people, with names
such as Nan, Bill, Kate and Burt. The film shows a horse first
being exercised, then led away from a burning stable; both
sequences having been treated and re-coloured; the transporta-
tion of the viewer back to the 1950's is achieved entirely successfully, largely thanks to production designer Eve Stewart's adept
use of dimly lit brick passageways and cramped doorways. I
certainly felt why cameraman Dick Pope emphasises advances
in social attitudes and living conditions that were largely won
by ordinary people. Language was central to the plot, where
barriers and miscommunication force the collapse of a relationship between writer Paul and his wife Camille, and their interac-
tion with American producer Prokosch, who speaks no French.
This defamiliarised language, the use of four different
tongues—French, English, German, Italian—force the viewer to
focus on the character's communicative methods as much as

what they actually said. The prostitution metaphor is employed with little subtlety, except in one brilliant moment. The football coach, about to pleasure himself with Isabelle, explains how Saint Etienne should have never sold Dominique Rocheteau, suggesting that both international superstars and sex trades alike are trapped within an economic superstructure that demands the sale of the self. More than any other work, this film transposed the spirit of early punk music into cinema. Cuba is introduced as a land of great beauty as recorded by Christopher Columbus. However, it is quickly revealed as far more complex than initially implied. Cuba's modernity is quickly established. The first story is set in a nightclub where American businessmen take an imperialist attitude toward the native women. The theme of capitalist oppression reaching into all walks of life is immediately forefronted, with this oppression leading from the intrusion of Westerners to the astonishing police brutality of the third and finally story, climaxing with the victory of the communist revolutionaries in a classically propagandistic scene of flags, songs, and smiles. The ethic of using such a serious subject in this sort of experiment are complex, but, crucially, the director ensures that human suffering is never downplayed. Although he said that this film is not aiming to depict the explicit, illegal life of gays in the Soviet Union, using the post-Stalinist criminalisation of homosexuality as a metaphor for censorship, the pain it shows is very real. Antonia San Juan's performance as Agrado, peeking in a brilliantly observed monologue on being an authentic transexual woman, was so good that people speculated intensely about her gender. She later said, 'I'm not a transvestite or transsexual, and that's all there is to say about that.' This film contains many of the director's obsessions, which would become familiar, featuring overtly sexualized women, drag queens, and New Wave counterculture in a screwball narrative in which Riza Nero, the gay son of the emperor of Tehran, disguises himself as a punk rock singer to avoid a group of terrorists, and forms his first heterosexual relationship with the nymphomaniac Sexillia. The opening shot of a man's crotch seen from Sexillia's perspective sets the tone with just the barest of restraint. The film's claustrophobic setting provides a wonderful combination of comedy and drama, and a great demonstration of how the scarcity of words inside a film, usually presented by intertitles or other written forms, increases their value. The moment when the husband and the printer see that the wife has departed is one of the most quietly heartbreaking intertitles in history. It is also obvious that the terrorists have no aim and no message. The director refuses to make any attempt to understand them, as many in the West struggled to do after 9/11, as the mainstream media denied any motive for their actions. The Iraq War, thought to have radicalised the London bombers of July 7th, 2005, and those whose attacks failed two weeks later, is never mentioned, although British troops remained in the country when the film was made. Fortunately, this film is fascinating as a historical record of Soviet economic policy and tantalising as an indication of how the avant-garde explored the possibilities of sound film, or the complex relationships between modernity, modern art and propaganda. It is not merely a historical artifact though. It is a relentlessly challenging, constantly fascinating film offering viewers an entirely unique visual, audible, and ontological experience. For students of radical film history, this film reads as a response to Chris Marker's three-hour documentary *A Grin Without a Cat*, made in 1977. Also comprised of archive footage and voiceover, this mediated dissipation of 60's and 70's struggles, cutting between France, Vietnam, Algeria, Bolivia, Cuba and Czechoslovakia at speed, giving a sense that the energy of the pending revolution persisted even as the movements themselves had been extinguished. I didn't appreciate the director using this method of distancing himself from the memories and emotions in his script in this way. I didn't initially see the humour in Snow reading the director's recollections of a photo taken in Snow's studio in 1965, recounting a disagreement over the typeface on a poster that the director had designed for an exhibition of Snow's art, concluding, quote, 'I regret to say Snow was right. I wish I could apologise to him.' The film cut from a hammer and a sickle to a Coca-Cola, from the Kremlin to the World Trade Centre, making the inference that a Cold War empire was propagated by opposing ideologies in similar ways. It was shot in Hollywood on an iPhone 5, which did not require a permit. Two painters, Rene Magritte and Salvador Dali, were impressed by the idea of camera angles and the combination of suspense. As well as placing a clock in all of the locations, the director punctuates the action with an hour countdown, capturing the rising urgency of its script, occurring, as the title suggests, over a single day. The protagonist's secret was crucial to the film's success in North America, as it's sympathetic portrayal of an IRA member was to its blunted reception in Britain. Especially as the IRA bombing campaign was in full swing in 1992. The director reflected that, because Anglo-Irish issues were less well understood in the US, the distributors could play up to the sexual politics creating a frenzy by begging the audience not to reveal the twist. The film was banned in Britain after the British Board of Film Classification called it 'So cryptic as to be almost meaningless,' and included that, 'If it has a meaning, it was doubtless objectionable.'

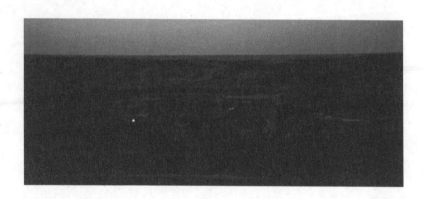

A Train in the Night Passing
(Schrift for the Liberated Nacht)
Anna Thew

How could I write this? Introducing no film, drafting a text, or
a Spiel, a play for no film, there'll be only a pixelated virtual film,
a fotocopy of a film—so I'll intro a *collage* film.

STOLEN TIME... *Film Fathoms, or the Revenge of the Lost Negatives*—rather the destroyed negatives—all the originals, A & B
rolls, sound masters, the lot—over 10 years of work, over 10
hours of film—half a life time—chucked on a skip in the digital
takeover of the last UK laboratory Soho Images, by Deluxe
142, UK registered, US subsidiary of the global digital media
giant Deluxe Inc., NY, owned by Pearlman, one of the 15 richest
guys in the US, with a finger in the arms + oil + art take over
pie, like Murdoch, like killer Cuadrilla, all linked, FRACKING
—NEWS—media—digital warfare—shit, the digital takeover
+ disruption of democracy—of socialism—of the collective
—STOLEN TIME—a progression from mending Dad's piano
—which lost fragments should I begin with—which pieces
I never finished from *Lao's Scroll* to *FACES* to *Amiamo Magnani*
—reverting to portraits, diary, landscape + cityscape and ruins...
I'd only just got over a 5 years legal wrangle with
Deluxe 142 trying to recover the pieces from *L.F.M.C.
Demolition* to *Autumn Rush for Kurt Kren* to *Fragments
for Eye Drift*—get the drift—*BROKEN PIECES*, as if
the trashing of our beloved Co-op in 2000 and all
our dreams wasn't enough—our cinema cum studio
cum workshop—a play room—so there's hard core
selectivity and dispelling the anger—so this film is
about revenge, rage, like dear Michael Brynntrup's
film, *Love, Jealousy and Revenge*, and I'm so stressed
by the current political situation that I can hardly
formulate a 10 minute presentation of shadows—the
fundamental difference between film + digital transmission—emission of static squares of pulsating
light—not spheres—film emulsion is like swirling
grains of sand or silver dust, physical spherical particles of colour in spiral formation—on each frame;
the grains shift like falling snow... I can't talk about
the digital takeover of film without talking about the
digital takeover of the archive and the invisibility,

availability facility disappearance, to introduce my
films that no longer exist as films, or films that I love
presenting—artists' films—film-makers' films—
Paul Sharits' *Razor Blades*—N.G. Smith's *Bird Xerox*
to Kenneth Anger's *Eaux D'Artifice*—well you know,
Kenneth said it was OK that I kept re-filming bits of
his films and pinching the crackled optical sound
as he STOLE a lot of footage anyhow and never had
the copyright for *Peggy Sue* or *Blue Velvet* or *Hit the
Road Jack* or Respighi's *The Fountains of ROME* for
Fireworks or Vivaldi's Concerto for *Eaux d'Artifice*. Be
my guest he said... as he defaced my forearm—so
I made a 2 minute ditty called *When Kenneth Anger
Signed My Arm, I Didn't Wash For A Week* and Deluxe
142 destroyed the negs for that too—meanwhile I love
camp theatrical films—the queer canon—like Balch
/ Burroughs' *The Cut Ups*, recently falling for Werner
Schroeter—*The Death of Maria Malibran* and *Palermo
oder Wolfsburg* or *Il Regno di Napoli*—like the best of
more underground—Fassbinder's *Satan's Brew* and
Matthias Müller's 80's *Aus der Ferne* and I love uncle
Kurt Kren + Stan the Man (Brakhage) but the broader Kren church with films like *10/65 Selbstverstüm-
melung*—self-mutilation w. Günter Brus or *6/64 Mama
Und Papa*. Otto Muehl when the Co-op pre the Lux
digital arts takeover started charging thro' the roof
for shorts and I had a special file of my own for Chelsea and FLUX with a stash of permissions to screen
at £1 per minute or for nothing. Bruce Baillie's *All My
Life, Mass for the Dakota Sioux, Castro Street*—any of
Kurt Kren, Chick Strand, Yann Beauvais—so I should
tell you of a few films I've screened over and over like
Descent of a Seductress of Jean Matthee, Jonas Mekas'
diary films *Lost, Lost, Lost...* and *Walden*—anything
by Warren Sonbert. *Betty Boop*, Oskar Fishchinger,
Joseph Cornell, Marie Menken, Anthony Balch, Jean
Genet's *Un Chant D'Amour*. *Chelsea Girls* if you can get
it. Taka IImura's *AI Love*, Peter Kubelka's *Arnulf Rainer*
or *Adebar und Schwechater*. Uncle Kurt's *37/78 Tree
Again*, *3/60 Bäume im Herbst* living in underground
celluloid history. Taka didn't turn up for his shadow
performance film at the old Co-op—he couldn't get

a visa like Moumen Smihi at the Tate—so I had to perform Taka's shadow film with the text for him *I Am a Viewer, You Are a Viewer*, and what I love is the performative aspect of film—actually physically lacing it, touching it—filming with a macro lens, with single frames—like discovery, like tucking into a box of coloured jewels—abstract treasure—"*Chance, chance, chance...,*" as Takehisa Kosugi said—so we filmed Piero della Francesca's *Madonna del Parto*—it's the only pregnant woman in art existence + they peeled her off the wall of the chapel in Monterchi + stuck her in a Museum behind glass—well they chucked that clandestine reel on a skip too—along with the footage of *Cine Ferrari* and *Waves* at Porto Ercole—why Porto Ercole?

Oh! Because Caravaggio was supposed to have died there, collapsed on the beach from malaria.

Collage—compartments of the mind. Mental short circuiting —random reading—Léger said that the only thing in film was movement, the cut—add the CLOSE-UP within the frame and from frame to frame—what Kubelka called the 'strong cut' as opposed to the seamless unmemorable imperceptible cut— our cuts are about collage, assemblage—disjunctive surprise —delight, rhythm + variation—gathering like notebooks....

And we can't resist a little chanson, rather ein Lied—
an adaptation of elderly Marlene Dietrich's Lili Marlene,
"Bei der Laterne vor dem Co-op Tor, steht ein Projektor
und steht er noch davor, Da wollen wir uns wiedersehen,
wenn wir bei dem Projektor stehen und die schöne silbere
Leinwand ansehen', wipe away a salty tear, "wie eins die
Anna und Steve und George..."
Steve Farrer and George Saxon,
The Three Musketeers

+ Pavement Via Manin
(Rome coming up)

Schrift randomly interspersed with diaries for diaries for film...

and not able to begin ?

6 days heat and travel, trains and brain death, mosquitoes, and discomfort!

I have this habit of wanting to begin each time on a separate page halfway thro'—if anyone opened the book they'd not know where to begin,

Think of a rhythm—draw to a fast, pulsating rhythm and this will end up like cutups or as fast as BLURT at least, or maybe faster.

Lurking and hanging about on street corners, cruising and twilight places with pink sky. Can they suppress the colour to make it like B/W?

Write to Caspar

   ....

select at least 20–30 pieces of text, some isolated words. wholly a construct.

It should be all excitement and forward looking with body pieces and good dark light
with plenty of camera movement to make the audience dizzy
like a dance piece, slow, slow, quick, quick, slow.

under the hedge, in a park, up against a garage wall—over the bonnet of a car.
thorough naughtiness. under the bed. the Pope on tele in the background.

I had another thought last night that various people would ex-pound in various languages like newsmen. the contrast between that and the action—getting from one thing to another through a door, in a train

a train in the night passing

by a train shed

225

the pavement...

Via Manin, ROMA

with the girl in trainers on the street outside, paced by an
Indian, paced by a crony, doddering, hardly able to stand but
still able to purchase. Both swing right, simultaneously moving
in on their prey like spiders, no, like grubs. The girl with long
curls and wide glazed eyes turns back along the pavement, arm
in arm with the wizened octogenarian, feet shuffling, clinging,
hardly able to stand, his head barely to her shoulder, as youths
titter and squirm with laughter, enough for a fix, past the tall
black woman with broad shoulders and a broad back, full six
feet topped with a tussled mane of thick black hair, bare backed,
silver slim blouse, barely to cover the tight red skirt and huge
heels towering above...

next in line, some tired and greasy shopkeeper with his wife at
home in front of the TV perhaps that's a puritan thought.

*diritto, se
scadenza.
i seguenti*

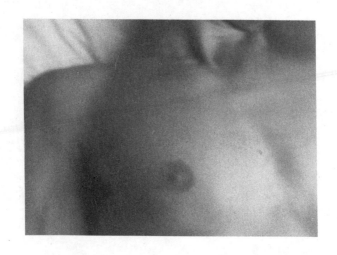

Here this pointless, flares of SNOW
broken, emulsion severed ripped
enjoyable the delight of play
far from the madding crowd
Playschool is here, *innerlich*,
inwardly *inhaltslos*,
David silhouetted against the
lurid green vortex of his own
making, stunned like a child
at its first wobbly line. drop-out
travelling, macroscopic channelling
like maggots in the machine,
that circuit boards consort with
shapes of Christmas packings,
it would be worth to account a bit
a slow zoom steady-handed
covert framing from start to end
careful diagonals—the man
like Aeneas boxing shadows with
surface emulsion crazed,

Zeno's arrow?

OSNABRÜCK '93, *David Larcher dishevelled, barefoot in leopard
skin tights, speaking into the microphone as* VIDEOVOID *is shown
publicly for the first time*

Sparrows squabbling in close
up. squawking, feathers flying
dark batting silhouetted against
the lens, fly away,
Soft focus blurred landscape
hissing.

A boy leaning against the wall
of a wooden barn, outside a
sloping hill, a forest.
a stable, straw. the stable boy
wanking

Chill frost.

this film is most beautifully
printed in black and white, soft
lit to silver, block black contrast
with starch white.
colour bursts through like a
spasm, relief scraping the
surface of the eye. like a
series of blemishes and explosions

PAINT without PAINT. the painted
face

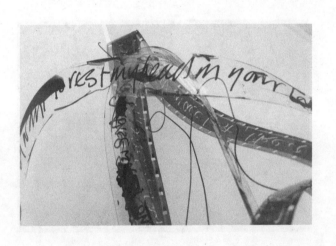

blossoms. deep red murmurs
viridian taint. sprinkled
like powder. a collapse
into the sofa of seeing. to be
alive again

no-one will see such a thing

Draft an outline three months
of finger printing and drawing
in thick pencils of charcoal

to childhood, childhood where
none of this happened and
expectations were still a miracle
and nonsense was alright.
intelligence not a question

Threads of music, draw together
all those things you like to have there
in one go. Start to build
a soundtrack for one part hesitant
mutterings.
Film music. Film music hesitantly
on the screen. Fellini's notebooks
the music is so enveloping.

A SCORE for something
the sound of squeaking metal
of squeaking swings.

—

Bagnena

Blank Page—3 years later
found heat again AGOSTO
storto empty headed. detached
staccata staccata toccata pizzicata
circondata ma sola—oh!
e non mi ricordo di niente, le
pre-occupazioni cancellate dal caldo,
cervello cucinato—cooked mind
insects creeping and crawling
lizards running, turquoise, blank,
bright rose heaven rose pluck word
by pool borghesia turquina e limpida.
lavender love lose losing
love nevver no. dog friends. dog roses
end game breeze lifts the dust dry
leaves and knot of pretensions as ants
crawl across my page of nothing
una pagina di niente. eh?

—

brittle bright blue green sparks of pool

shuttle against the deep rose red of
petals, lips parted not the sign of
time, roughness of sun blisters, flecks
sweat, hairs, mist, and distance of
infantility long gone, I am about
to return grace lost, like a brush against
the wall heat dried with an ant hill
of memories

man side / eyes skinned

eye-like—(like), like
dry things that bite and blood suck
fuzz and flurry of insect industry a
tickling underlife on hot rock

not to write is to be found—some secret
caper through my book caught you red
hot fingered eye full of ring sparkle.

oh, what fun it is with a handwritten film washing line...

> *... and the soundtrack by the way is from* STOLEN TIME
> *proper with my Dad's piano having a new action put
> in it and the track has Vatche Jambazian in concert play-
> ing Galina Ustvolskaya and ends with him and Vasilis
> Rakitzis hyping up a Schubert Fantaisie duet ...*

FIN

Sigourney Weaver
(She Takes Control of the Situation)
Adam Christensen

Belles and Bell ends, it's that time of the month again; the Liberated Film Club at Close-Up, London's only cinema. As you may well know, neither the guest nor the audience know the film that will be screening. My name is Stanley Schtinter, and I cannot be with you tonight, but I can tell you that in September, we have Laura Mulvey at the Liberated Film Club; in October, Astra Taylor at the Liberated Film Club; and November, Dennis Cooper at the Liberated Film Club. But tonight, we have the indominable, the impeccable, the fabulous Adam Christensen.

[Wild applause]

But, first, ~~the dictator~~ director of the Liberated Film Club, Mundo Schtinter.

[Further into the wild]

Um, my apologies ladies and gentlemen. It seems that Mundo cannot be with us tonight. Although I understand he has prepared a special dedication for Adam and we have a stand-in? Ok, um... Ok, ok. Ladies and gentlemen, boys and girls, belles and bell ends, please welcome—first to the stage tonight—George Michael.

Kindness
In your eyes, I guess
You heard me cry
You smiled at me
Like Jesus to a child

I'm blessed
I know
Heaven sent
And Heaven stole
You smiled at me
Like Jesus to a child

And what have I learned
From all this pain
I thought I'd never feel the same
About anyone
Or anything again

But now I know
When you find your love
When you know that it exists
Then the lover that you miss
Will come to you on those cold, cold nights

Ladies and gentlemen, Adam Christensen...

[Christensen performed a song. The following extract is from a conversation with Schtinter, recorded in Creixomil, Portugal.]

The first time Jordan and I had sex he didn't know who Sigourney Weaver was. And I was like... *Alien?* And he said 'Well, I guess I've seen that one.' And I just showed him, like, *Alien Resurrection*, with Winona Ryder, and it is very camp, over the top, lesbian... When Winona gets shot, Weaver puts her hand inside Winona's body and there's all of this white juice, and she, like, sticks her finger inside and says 'You're a robot?!' And it's really great with all of this white goo and Sigourney Weaver's fingers, and at the same time she's not normal human anymore, she's also like a mix between human and alien and like this woman that thinks she's woman but is also a mix with a robot... it's really quite amazing. And then, so I did an edit of Sigourney Weaver and Jamie Lee Curtis movies together, and it's really impossible to show because there's lots of like copyright issues, if you want to show it in a 'proper' space... and then I like to dance with it with a massive flat screen, where the hole in the body is your own body and she's like sticking her finger inside you... 90s Sigourney Weaver is really amazing. She was in *Copycat*. You watched *Copycat*? It came out in the same year as *Seven*, and *Seven* was the cool one. And it's okay but it's annoying. Really gritty, male... the destruction of a really beautiful relationship or something. And then you're like...

I don't know, it's just a bit too much. Whereas hers was really her—over-the-top-camp—and it's based around these female characters instead of these men-characters being all like... '*Yeah being in the big city is quite hard 'cause I can't really like keep the relationship together and I'm working all the time and she's home and alone and she's pregnant and now she's getting killed by a serial killer I'm investigating...*;' whereas the other one is more like, '*I'm a scientist... I'm researching serial killers and then suddenly these serial killers get a fetish around me, like, they wanna kill me and I'm investigating them and like FUCK THEM and then oh sorry suddenly it was actually a really close call and now I'm having a trauma and moving outside of her flat makes her have all of these anxieties...*' and it was also around the time that I realised the anxieties

I was having were things that were deeper to do with
your anatomy and your brain, and I was using all
of that anxiety produced in these hyped up movies
to project, to realise... Well, it was really funny.

In the opening scene she's really confident
giving a lecture, then there's an attempted murder
attempt, a psycho killer, and she's wearing a red dress,
of course, and gets choked in the toilet, um, and
then... Holly Hunter suddenly is the investigator of
a new crime in the near future, and so Weaver tries to
help her because she's being involved somehow by
all of this virtual reality thing, she's in her flat always
on her computer, and it becomes all about modern
computers... but 90s modern computers, with paused
screens, digitalised fish moving across... and like images coming out, really bad images, 'LETS TRY AND
LOCATE WHERE THIS VIDEO CAME FROM AND
OH MY GOSH A LINK HAS BEEN BROKEN' this kind
of thing... It's really good.

So, there's a new serial killer out on the move,
and is he connected somehow to that guy that tried to
kill her, because she's being involved somehow, and
is he that guy in prison somehow like puppeteering
the whole thing... it's quite nice... and all the women
are amazing... and the male detectives are also amazing, and all the villains over the top camp, unrealis-
tic... MTV villains in a sense, I really like it for that; it's
quite hard when you first watch it and you're like no,
no; *Seven* is obviously the better film, but I remember Sigourney Weaver saying 'Yeah *Seven* is okay but
Copycat is the movie you watch *really*,' and now I
completely understand that; that is a movie that I've
watched hundreds of times.

It never gets boring.

It's really good.

And the relationship between Holly Hunter
and Sigourney Weaver is quite amazing.

And the end? Um, it's a repeat of the scene
that opens the films but it's the other guy trying to
recreate the... so she's wearing the red dress and he's
trying to choke her in the toilets and then... I don't
actually remember.

Of course, it ends well.

She survives, again.

But this time she really takes control of it.

While he's choking her, she just starts laughing.

Saying *Bahahaha it's pathetic you shit!* It's quite good.

It's amazing.

She takes control of the situation.

Did you ever watch *Death and the Serpent*? No? *Death and the Maiden*, it's called. A horrible director. The paedophile one? What's his name? Polanski, yeah. So, like, he did... Polanski did a version of the theatre play with her in it, and it had also... the actor who played Ghandi? Ben Kingsley. He's amazing. And he plays this man in need of a car being fixed and she's like... 'That's the guy who tortured me! Now I re-member!' and that film with *Copycat*—and with, uh, *Alien Resurrection*—they're very similar in their 90s language. They even have similarities in the narra-tives; in scenes... You can immediately cut from a scene in *Copycat*, being anxious in the flat, to a scene to *Death and the Maiden*, anxious in the flat, with a knife, and it's the wrong way to say that she's not an amazing actress, no, but... she doesn't make you feel her pain in a traditional way, just in a different way. I don't know what it is but there's something about the failure in it that makes you feel her pain. I find it very interesting. There's something really real about them at the same time as being really very constructed.

Maybe we can watch them, and you tell me what you think?

It's 'cause I was also interested in the masculine female characters of Hollywood movies, like Jamie Lee Curtis. They're both extremely tall and so they have problems with doing diversity in Hollywood, so when it comes to like... horror-action to family roman-tic comedies. They can do mothers, but not really in a way because they're not like heterosexual normative honey-mummy as such and very rarely do they do ro-mantic comedies because they're basically a head higher than any of those men that they're supposed to be opposite... Ah, it's so funny that whole thing, the whole construction.

Make me stop talking; make me stop...

[Many dogs start barking in the distance]

Why are all the dogs always outside at night in Portugal? I just don't get it. They're making them live their natural life. They should not. They should sleep at night and be awake in the day. Natural times.

[Impersonates dog; responds to the far-out barks]

In Turin. No, not Turin. Napoli. In Napoli I was really ill with a fever and I thought a long walk to the big volcano would be an amazing idea. I'd already walked two and a half hours to the village of the volcano, and then started walking up. Italian men were driving around in cars. I was the only one walking. And then every apartment on the road on the way up the volcano has crazy dogs barking and they sound really vicious... and I was sweating so much with this fever, I had to sit down, I sat on the dried out black lava. And I realised I really needed a shit, so I made a shit on the lava, and it was really brown compared to the lava, the black tar... and so I sat there with a cigarette and all of the burnt trees and decided 'Okay I'm going to give up—I can't do the top.' So, I started walking back and all of the dogs had broken out because they were so pissed off about this person walking up the hill, and suddenly they're out on the road ready for me when I came down, and they're all coming at me, going for me, and I had to do this crazy Italian like *'I'll fucking kill you, stay where you are.'* And they were like, *'Okay, he's the boss.'* The problem was that some of them became so impressed with my authority that they became my pals walking down the mountain. And then a police car approached and stopped me and said 'So, you with your dogs... what's all this about?' And I said I have nothing to do with it. And then they left but it was sort of scary because

I thought they could turn on me any minute, like *'You aren't the boss here, actually. You aren't boss enough. We're looking through the rubbish, why aren't you looking through the rubbish? You aren't the boss, are you!'*

I didn't get paid for that job either.

Desert, again. A man and child walk together, and sing.

Laura,
Is the face in the misty light
Footsteps, that you hear down the hall
The laugh that floats
on a summer night
That you can never quite recall
And you see Laura
On a train that is passing through
Those eyes, how familiar they seem
She gave your very kiss to you
That was Laura, but she's only a dream

I was born in 1941 into wartime Britain. As I spent the first six years of my life in the country, I saw no moving images whatsoever; there was no access to the cinema in the Sussex countryside and obviously no TV. Even when my family moved back to London after the war, we only occasionally went to the cinema so, in these circumstances, I can remember quite clearly the first films I saw. Recently I realised that four particular scenes from my childhood filmgoing had left a kind of afterimage in my memory. Furthermore, not only are they visually connected but they also strangely prefigure, as it were, my much later (1990s) fascination with the film fragment. Here I want to try to reconstruct the four scenes and why they made such an impression on me as a child and why these afterimages still mean something to me now.

The first film I saw was *Nanook of the North*, probably because my father, who was Canadian, had a special interest in Inuit communities. He had travelled up the Mackenzie River to the Arctic Circle and spent some time living with 'Eskimos,' as they were then called, before joining the army and coming to England during the war. There must have been some revival of *Nanook* in London in the late 40s. The second film, more conventionally, was *The Red Shoes*, released in 1948 so around and about then. By that time my sister and I were (primitively but enthusiastically) taking ballet dancing classes and for us, as for so many other ballet mad little girls of our generation, *The Red Shoes* was an obvious and very special treat. In 1951 we went to see Renoir's *The River*, which would have had a double appeal. Once again, in the first instance, it was parental: when my mother was at Oxford in the late twenties, she had become a dedicated cinephile, recording the films she saw in a notebook, and Renoir was a particular favourite of hers. Rumer Godden's novella would have been a further appeal: a group of girls, their friendships, their rivalries, first love etc., in the exotic and strange Indian setting. (Also, around and about 1951, for reasons that I won't go into here, my mother took us to *An American in Paris*. Although it was an extremely memorable experience, it didn't leave an 'afterimage'.) The final film came later: Buñuel's *Robinson Crusoe*. When it came out in London in 1954, I was taken with a school friend by his very sophisticated mother. I must have seen quite a few other movies by then, but *Robinson Crusoe* is the last in the series of films that I want to talk about here.

The films, *Nanook*, *The Red Shoes*, *The River* and *Robinson Crusoe* all remained vaguely in my memory. But it was only when I was thinking about stillness and the moving image, about the cinematic fusion of the animate and the inanimate (the thoughts that finally coalesced into *Death 24× a Second*) that these four moments of uncanniness came back to me, returning strong visual images that had persisted across a later lifetime of filmgoing. So, this is what happened: as I rediscovered these early memory traces, they seemed to chime with the more theoretical interests of my approximately forty-five-year older self, which I superimposed retrospectively.

First of all, there is the image of *Nanook* as he struggles with a fish that he's caught through a hole in the ice, but he can't succeed in landing. He clings to his rod and line; his body, in my memory at least, is jerked about, his movements losing their normal continuum and smoothness. Furthermore, the force acting upon him is invisible and in a certain sense mysterious. In my retrospective imagination, Nanook's de-naturalised figure seemed embody, on the screen, the jerky movement of celluloid as it runs through the projector. It seemed as though the optical effect, the phi phenomenon, with which the projector creates the cinema's illusion of movement and streamlines the human body on screen, had suddenly lost its efficacy.

Secondly, for many years, the only image that I retained from *The Red Shoes* comes from the ballet 'The Red Shoes.' Vicky dances through a fairground into an increasingly surreal and fantastic setting. Suddenly, a piece of newspaper is picked up by the wind; it mutates into the shape of a man, who dances away with her. The paper man never becomes an actual man; he hovers between the shape of a human and his original substance. For me, (again retrospectively) this figure materialised the cinema's uncanny blurring of the animate and the inanimate, a reminder that the appearance of human movement on the screen is a fantastic illusion created by the succession of still frames that run through the projector. Jean Epstein said of cinema: 'a transformation as amazing as the generation of life from inanimate things.'

Thirdly, *The River*. Surprisingly, the scene that stayed in my memory had nothing to do with the film's romance, with the teenage girls and their first loves. I remembered the little boy's fascination with a cobra that he tries to tame by playing a pipe and bringing offerings of milk. The cobra lives in the roots of an enormous tree and, when it finally emerges, its long, curled shape seems to bring to life the long stretches of root that made up its home. Once again: a fusion between the animate and the inanimate but one that's enhanced uncannily by the boy's wonder at this mysterious creature. While he might hope to tame the cobra, he also treats it like a god, and it will ultimately kill him.

Finally, *Robinson Crusoe*. In the scene that stayed with me, Crusoe creates a scarecrow to protect his crops. Somehow (I don't remember, I haven't re-seen the film) he has found women's clothes, which he uses to transform the scarecrow into a female companion. As Crusoe fondles and embraces the wooden object, my twelve-year-old self was both shocked and fascinated. This moment retrospectively resonates for me with my later self's psychoanalytic interest in the fetishisation of the female body in and through cinema. Ultimately, the mechanics of cinema and the mechanics of male desire work together, not to bring the desired object to life, but to contain it in the uncanny uncertainty of the beautiful automaton.

All these figures have some relation to the cinema's fusion of the animate and the inanimate, which in turn leads to the process of film projection. The projector was always the most repressed and the most mysterious of industrial cinema's machines. Clunky and unsightly, it was hidden away at the back of the auditorium. But it was the true source of the cinema's magic: tricking the human eye to create the illusion of movement as the series of individual frames are transformed into a stable and continuous flow. Now, in the digital era, invisibility has been overtaken by disappearance and the projector gains poignancy as its use fades into history. These memories are a conscious tribute to the way the magic of the projector, somehow or other, seems to have seized hold of my childhood unconscious between the formative ages of six and twelve.

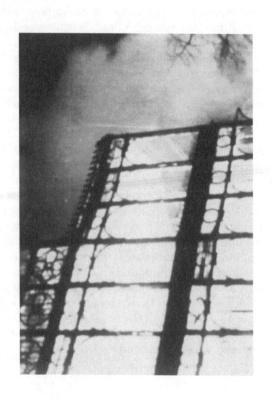

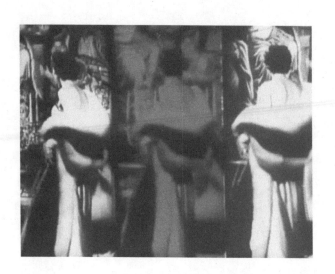

The only thing that I don't like about coming to this side of the pond is that my name reminds everyone of a car. Thank you for having me at this mysterious event. Thank you, Gareth, for being such a wonderful host and drawing me into this mayhem.

I am not much of a cinema watcher so when I was thinking about how to introduce film in general, I thought, I'm actually uniquely ill-equipped to do this. I already told Stanley this will be one of three or four films I watch this entire year. So, it will be memorable.

I'm here with a film called *What is Democracy?* and a book about democracy, so... a part of being the democracy is being the collective. In the film, I'm asking people what they think and there's a focus on the collective consciousness—what do people think about ideas? So today I thought it would be interesting to get into our collective unconscious, and also to create a collective out of this room. So, what I want us to do is tell a story together about what we think this magnificent film might be: a kind of exquisite corpse thing. But what I really want to do is tap into the film we're going to see, and I knew that this was the right thing to do because downstairs there's actually a poster for *Exquisite Corpse*, so it's already happening, and if you'll just believe we'll be able to find some magic together.

Everyone is going to say one word and we're going to tell a story until I decide that it's over; we're going to go through the crowd and back around if the story's not over. And I want us to think in terms of collectivity. Let's let our words interconnect, maybe even recurring characters (if we are to be so conventional as to have characters). Let's work together to create something. Get into the cinematic mode. We're going to write a script together. What do you think the story might be? Try to get your mind in synch with everybody else in the room. Okay, so I'm going to begin with a word and then my friend David here will begin...

THERE
WAS
HE

SORRY?

WHY
NOT
DO
FIELD
APPLE
IS

WORK TOGETHER PEOPLE!

AND
YOU
LETTUCE
WORK
APART
FROM
IF
I
CLOSE
THE
BOXES
TOGETHER
HOWEVER
SOMETIMES
TACTILIUM
ROSE
WHATEVER
STANLEY
YEAH
COMES
TO
YOU
IS
MY
OH SORRY BRUV
INTERESTING
ENOUGH

                                              FOR
                                            AMPLE
                                              GYM
                                             WHAT

WHAT DO YOU MEAN?
APPLE WHAT?
I'M NOT IN CHARGE?
WHO'S NEXT?

                                                I
                                             WILL
                                            THINK
                                            ABOUT
                                             THIS
                                            THING
                                               IN
                                               MY
                                             MIND
                                           CALLED
                                        POLITICAL
                                          REALITY
                                            SEEPS
                                         THROUGH
                                           GUTTER
                                           BEFORE
                                         BECOMING
                                          GERMAN
                                          BANANAS
                                        HALLOUMI
                                        TOGETHER
                                           INSIDE
                                          ANOTHER
                          UH, PART OF THE, UH . . .
                                             HEAD
                                             BUTT
                                             THEN
                                               IT
                                             CAME
                                            LIONS

266

WHAT?
IT CAME?
WHAT?

                              I UNDERSTOOD IT *TAMED* LIONS?

OH
OKAY
COOL

                                          MUSCLE
                                            OR
                                         THEY
                                      KNOW
                      UH, THEY, UH, WAIT, NO
                                    WERE
                                      ALSO
                                  VAGRANT
                                HARMLESS
                                      AND
                                      WHY
                                MATTER
                                NOTHING
                                    ELSE
                              HAPPENED
                              SUDDENLY
                                      IN
                                    THE
                                  ROAD
                              DECANTED
                                        A

A?
ANYTHING YOU WANT, AN A?
REALLY?

                                          SEA-

SEA?

                                        WHAT
                                      WHEN

                                    EVER
                         UH, YES, UH, YES
                                SOMEBODY
                                  WANTED
                                 KNOWING
                                   JENNY

OH! WE HAVE A CHARACTER?
FINALLY—
JENNY?

                                   LOVES
                     OH LOVES, JENNY LOVES
                                 BOOTLEG
                                BOOTLEG?
                        SHE LOVES BOOTLEG?
                                   SMALL
                                  SMALL?
                                     YET
                                POWERFUL
                                   APPLE
                                     AND
                              HEARTBREAK
                                 BLOCKED
                                      WE
                                   ABOUT
                              WEE ABOUT?
                                   JENNY
                            TRANSGRESSES
                            INCIDENTALLY
                                    FISH
                                   FISH?
                                   FRUIT
                               THE HORSE

THAT'S TWO WORDS...
AND FRUIT THE HORSE?

                                   HORSE
                                    FISH
                                  CALLED

A FISH CALLED?

A FISH CALLED AND UH, UM...

SO, THE FISH CALLED MAYBE AND UH, WELL
FOUND
IN
ANY

THAT'S IT
THE END

I sort of had this other idea about what this was. I thought that we were going to stand up here, and then he was going to come up and whisper in my ear the name of the film, and then I was going to introduce the film. It was going to be a film he probably liked, or something like a film I didn't know, but that I would at least have the title. But now I understand that that's not the case, and that we're all in the dark. [laughter] So, I wasn't really prepared that I would just like talk. [laughter] And I'm not really like a talk-y person. So, I don't know what to do except that I can just pretend that you have all just asked me 'What are you doing lately?' [light laughter] I don't know what else to talk about. So, I'm just going to talk about stuff. So, I was just in Los Angeles for about two-and-a-half weeks. I'm from there, if you can't tell from my voice. But I'm from there. I was there because it was Halloween. I was there because I had made films with Zac Farley. We made two films, and we're starting to work on our new film. We're starting to raise money for a new film. The film is about a French family who puts on a home haunt. I don't think most of you probably know what a home haunt is. Most people don't. So, what is it, is it's like a tradition, phenomena in the United States, where a family, their kids—their neighbours will sometimes chip in—will turn their house into a haunted house. They decorate their house, and they put up props, and they make mazes inside their houses. They work very hard on them. Sometimes for a year. And they play the monsters, and their kids play the monsters. They charge people in the neighbourhood, or sometimes they advertise it on social media, and they'll say we're doing whatever it's called... Stone Point Cemetery, or... Twisted Minds Presents: Coven Escape or Salem Escape from the Coven. Then people will come see these things, then they'll come over and pay you whatever—5 pounds or something—and they'll walk through these haunted houses. So, we're going to make a movie about a French family that puts on a home haunt in France. I don't know how many of you are French, but the French really don't know very much about Halloween. They only know the most superficial things about Halloween. But they certainly don't know what a home haunt is, or what a haunted house attraction is. So, everybody in their little town... they live in a rural area, hence they are completely out of their minds, which it turns out they are. But they never say anything like 'What is this?' They don't know whether to be scared on embarrassed. In the film, they construct this haunted house in their house, and then, at the end of the film, people show up and they go through the haunted house, and all kinds of horrible things happen. Anyway, to research it we went to Los Angeles, because Los Angeles is like the king of the home haunt. There were like 70 of them. Zac and I went to like 39 of them. We spent like two weeks going to 39 of these things, every single night, from ones that people make in their houses all the way up to the really professional ones. Because Universal Studios and theme parks will make these very expensive mazes. Universal Studios does these Halloween haunt event where they build a maze with a million-dollar budget. So, we went through 39 of them, and talked to the people who made them. It was interesting. So that's what I was doing. Wow—okay. Yeah, so I did that [laughter]. That's all I did really. I saw some friends. I saw a movie I really hated called *The Lighthouse*. So, that's what I did. And then I came back to France. Another thing I'm doing is I'm co-writing a television show for this channel called Arte, which is like this German / French cultural channel. We're writing a three-episode television series that's going to be directed by Gisèle Vienne, who is this choreographer, director. She's going to direct the series, and Zac and I are writing the series. We've been working on it for five years. It was fun for about a year. Now it's been just horrible because I've never worked in television before, and I'm never going to work in television again. Because even though Arte is 'Art-y,' they're very much like the other television studios. You have to have suspense. When your characters do something, it has to pay off. You have to see their psychological development through the series and stuff. Lots of things we were not interested in doing, which is now in the script. It's been really horrible. All kinds of horrible things happened. Not to bring you down, but... We wrote it for this actress, this performer, a ventriloquist named Kirsten. We wrote it for her. It's about a ventriloquist, a woman who is a ventriloquist. She very, very loosely based on Candice Bergen, if you know who Candice Bergen is; who, as well as being an actress, was the daughter of Edgar Bergen. And, when I was a little kid, Edgar Bergen was like as famous as Elvis Presley. I mean, he was a ventriloquist, and he was like you can't even imagine how famous he was. In movies and television every day, and *da-da-da*. He died, and Candice Bergen... in the TV show, this woman who is the most famous ventriloquist in the world who died, she grew up being extremely jealous of this puppet, this dummy. It's named Franky. It was really famous and got all of her dad's attention. As a kind of cruel thing, he left the dummy to her. So, she now lives in this house, and she's gone kind of crazy, and she actually thinks it's a real person. She lives with this puppet, and it's like her son. So, that's the show. We made it for this ventriloquist named Kirsten Daly, based on her own dummy. It was based on her talent. We worked on it for four years, and she got cancer, and she died in August, suddenly. She was 38 or something. That's like the beginning of the curse. That was horrible personally, as well as for the show. Ever since then it's been hell. So, now I'm doing this TV show that I hate, and I hate everything about it. I don't even know if it's going to happen anymore. We have a big meeting on Monday, where we have to try to convince the... The thing is, right before she got sick and died, we had to shoot a test shoot of three scenes. Three days before we shot the test shoot, she was told she had very serious cancer. And it's a comedy. She was not in the mood to do a comedy, and she is really brilliant, but did a really, really not correct performance in the test shoot. But then, we thought she was going to be okay. Then she died a week later. One of those crazy things. So, we had to make test footage for Arte because they had spent $50,000 on it. We had to turn in the test shoot, and they hated it. They said, 'This is not funny.' And we were like, 'She was dying.' They were like, 'I don't care, it's not funny.' So, now we have to convince them that it's funny. [laughter] We've been working on it for five years, and they still haven't said yes. If they don't say yes, I don't know what we're going to do. It's going to be like one of those things in the United States, one of those mass-shooting things. [laughter, someone shouts something from the audience] Yeah, but it's hard though. You get caught. So, have I been doing anything else? I am jetlagged really bad. I was waking up at 2 o'clock in the morning and going to bed at five o'clock at night. I didn't get to see Mark's show. I haven't really been doing much else. I finished a novel. It's good.

AUDIENCE MEMBER #1: What's the novel about?

It's about my friend George Miles. You know, I wrote these books called the *George Miles* cycle. There were like five books. Part of them were published in '89 and '91 and 2008. And they were for my friend George Miles, who was sort of a big, important person to me, and he ended up killing himself really young. It was a terrible thing. So, I wrote this book about my friendship with him. That's what the book is about. It's called... I don't know, does anyone else have any ideas?

AUDIENCE MEMBER #2: Your film?

Oh yeah. It's about a haunted house. We're trying to raise money for it. I mean, we will raise money for it. We just applied for some grant. We have €70,000 from the United States, from a foundation. But we probably need 200,000 to make it. I think, probably. So, we have to raise some more.

AUDIENCE MEMBER #3: Come on people!

[Laughter]

Cough up! Cough up!

AUDIENCE MEMBER #2: How much do you need? We'll buy lottery tickets.

AUDIENCE MEMBER #3: See, Shoreditch. Don't worry about it.

Yeah, we don't need very much money. We're making it... it's all in one house. The home haunt, as I explained, is really amateurish. It's all homemade, so the movie won't cost much to make. That's kind of our goal, to not make a movie that's too expensive, because, you know, we don't want to compromise and make something terrible, like *The Lighthouse*.

AUDIENCE MEMBER #1: I'm so sorry. How many times has your work been adapted?
By other people?

AUDIENCE MEMBER #1: Yeah.

Well, there's this horrible movie called *Frisk*. It was made in the early 90's. It was so horrible, that I wouldn't let anybody adapt anything for a long time because it was such a terrible experience. There's been some short films. I wrote a book called *God Jr.*, which is like my *nice* novel. They were going to do a film of it, but they didn't. Other than that, I think that's it. I don't know. I'm also just not interested in that. I mean, I'm sort of like 'It's a book.' It was meant to be a book, and it's all about a reader. It's all about the reader being in love with the book, and the language and imagination make the world. So, making it into a movie just seems like a bad idea. So, I don't know. Maybe somebody else can... That's it.

Yeah, so you're going to see a film. I have no idea what it is. All I know is that it's a film that you almost for absolutely sure haven't seen before. I think you almost absolutely for sure will never see again. [laughter] I really thought like, 'He's going to play *Salò* or something.' Or, like, 'Oh no, he's going to pick Bresson,' or he's going to pick something that I really hate, like Lars Von Trier. [laughter] But no, so I don't know what it is, and I don't think it's anything like that. So, I don't know. Anyway, I don't know if that's like enough. Is that enough?

'Cause I don't know what else to say.

I'm so sorry.

Perhaps you'd like to find out what this is.

[An audience bays]

LADIES, GENTLEMEN and NON-CONFORMULISTS. First to the stage tonight, and to introduce our special guest Stewart Home, its Alan Titchmarsh.

[The horticulturalist crosses the stage; music plays on; the horticulturalist sings]

Me and Stewart Home
We got a thing goin' on
We both know that it's wrong
But it's much too strong
To let it go now
We meet every day at the same cafe
Six-thirty and no one knows she'll be there
Holding hands, making all kinds of plans
While the jukebox plays our favourite songs

STEWART HOME: Thanks. I'm actually Mrs. Jones, pretending to be Stewart Home, but never mind... And obviously I was asked to come tonight because I wrote this book about Bruceploitation, *Re-Enter the Dragon: Genre Theory, Brucesploitation and the Sleazy Joys of Lowbrow Cinema*; you can buy one off me at the end of the show for ten quid (they're normally fifteen) so that's a bargain. And so, I'm gonna introduce this film, but I'd prefer to do it in a different way, see, not standing on my feet (*because* I am Mrs. Jones). So...

[Home is now standing on his head]

We all know that Bruceexploitation films turn the world upside down and, uh, Hegel got it all back to front as well, which is why Feuerbach and Marx had to stand him on his feet, and we all know there's a close relationship between exploitation film and avant-garde film, so the film you're going to see tonight is called *Bruce Against Iron Hand*, it's also sometimes called *Bruce Against Iron Finger*, and it stars the least interesting of the Bruce Lee clones, Bruce Li (spelt LI), although I much prefer Bruce Le (spelt LE, only one E not two EE's as in Bruce Lee), so this starts with some shenanigans at night, with a murder, and then we cut to Bruce Li coming into Hong Kong for his holidays, meeting up with some cops he knows (because he's a cop), and they go to a nightclub, and—of course—the band are miming to the Incredible Bongo Band's 'Bongolia,' because this is from 1979, and you find a lot of the music on these films is taken from what would become the classic sounds of hip-hop. The band is miming very badly; you can tell they're not *really* the Incredible Bongo Band; uh, and, of course, this invokes the Lettrist Cinema where Isou, and those around him in the early 50s, talked about dissociating sound and image in film, you know, a new experimental way of looking at film. A lot of these ideas were taken up by the French new wave, the Nouvelle Vague, but people like Chris Marker and Godard were doing a very commercial version of what the Lettrist's had done in the early-fifties, kind of selling out to mainstream cinema, which is not what Bruceexploitation does, because it NEVER strives to become mainstream cinema. The plot in *Bruce Against Iron Hand* is that people are being murdered by someone who's a master of the iron finger technique, and Bruce Li is investigating this, and there are two main suspects; Bruce Liang, who you'll remember from *The Dragon Lives Again*, the 1977 film where Bruce Lee wakes up in hell, played by Bruce Liang, sorry, purgatory, well, in the underworld, anyway, and he has to team up with Popeye and Kwai Chang Caine from *Kung Fu* and various other pop-cultural figures to fight the Exorcist and the Godfather and James Bond who are trying to run a racket in the underworld; and you'll all remember the classic opening scene where Bruce hasn't actually woken up in the underworld, and he's got his nun-chucks in his pants, and people get excited by the size of something this might indicate, but it's just his nun-chucks (rather disappointingly) but anyway, Bruce Liang gets to wear a red tracksuit—a little like Bruce Lee in those episodes of *Long Street*, the TV series, if you've seen that; and, um, the other main suspect is Ku Feng, who is in fact the murderer, and the reason he's doing these murders is he has a nymphomaniac girlfriend played by a Japanese actress called Lee Hoi-Gei, and she's going and picking up other men and he gets jealous because *his* particular brand of iron finger training means that if he has sex he'll die, so he's become a kung fu master, but he can't have sex anymore, so Hoi-Gei is picking up men and he's killing them, and the most spectacular instance of this happens at two-thirds into the film, and Hoi-Gei has got a guy who she's riding as a pony and he's in his swimming trunks and she's in her underwear and she's riding him like a pony and slapping his butt whilst 'Pusher Man' by Curtis Mayfield is playing in the background. Sorry, I need to stand up, otherwise I'm not going to finish this...

So, 'Pusher Man' is playing on the soundtrack, which obviously you'll all associate that with that (famous) montage of still photographs of drug-dealing from *Super Fly*, so it's a rather bizarre moment, and after about thirty seconds of this, she stubs her cigarette out in the guy's mouth who's doing the pony-play, and then her boyfriend turns up, so the guy jumps outta the window, but Ku then gets a hold of him, kills him, and then he kills his girlfriend, but before she dies she tells the cops what's going on, Bruce Li and Bruce Liang then run down to the docks and, in a typical Hong Kong cargo container scene, they fight it out with the bad guy and win in the end, of course. So, a pretty incredible film, and there's a pretty incredible story about how we got the 35mm print of this, you can watch the film on YouTube, and I do recommend it, but it's much better to see the 35mm print we have. [Home picks up the tin] You'll probably recall that when Severin released two Blu-Ray's of kung fu trailers, found in an old cinema that's now the Cube Cinema, in Bristol, and it turned out that someone had left a load of kung fu film trailers in this place, but also—secretly—and what Severin don't know (in spite of the fact that they interviewed me for their Brucesploitation special that's coming out soon, is that I was doing work at the Cube, showing stuff, again—harking back to Lettrism-things like my 2002 remake of *Screams in Favour of De Sade*, Debord's film which basically remakes *Has The Film Already Started* by Maurice Lemaître crossed with *L'Anti-Concept* by Gil J. Wolman. *Has The Film Already Started*—the first half of the film is silent, and it's the noise of the audience that constitutes the soundtrack, and it's a cut-up, really, of the ends of other films. And *L'Anti-Concept* was made to be projected onto a helium balloon, it consists of only black and white, and there's a soundtrack about the leftists and the people involved in the movement. Those were both made in '51 and in '52, and Debord made *Screams in Favour of De Sade*, where he has longer periods of blackness and silence in his film, and short bursts of light, and the final twenty-four minutes is entirely black and silent, and so obviously what Debord was doing was turning cinema back into theatre because it was the reaction of the audience that really counted. I remade that according to the logic of Hollywood, on its fiftieth anniversary, 2002, I made it in colour, so I had TV colour bars, rather than white, and I made it in English. People at the time, before the internet had really got going, I mean, it was going, but people didn't check everything out on it, they really... There were some people that didn't really believe that I would've, you know, wasted my time remaking this film, but if you don't believe me take a look at UbuWeb and you can see my remake of *Screams in Favour of De Sade*. But anyway, I guess we're lucky that this copy of *Bruce Against Iron Hand*—which again, is available on YouTube; and again, is an avant-garde classic—is available in this 35mm print that I dug up when I was at the Cube and, uh, stole from Severin, because the films were given to them—the rest of the material—so enjoy. And make sure you watch lots of other Brucesploitation classics, because this is the real avant-garde.*

*It is worthy of mention that *Bruce Against the Iron Hand* was not screened as a part of the evening's program.

A Letter from the Curator

*The second season of the Liberated Film Club prematurely conclud-
ed with the governmental instruction that all unnecessary social
contact should cease, as of 16/03/2020, and the subsequent 'stay at
home' order that followed, 23/03/2020. To signal the end of the series,
Schtinter mailed a letter to all regular and recent attendees, speaking to the death, rebirth, and re-death of the Club.*

20/03/2020 was to be the final date of the Liberated Film Club in its familiar unfamiliar format. I decided some months ago to end the Club's better-known manifestation to avoid it becoming a victim of its own success. *If* in the months to come our cinemas re-open, perhaps I will pick it up again, diluting the concept and betraying her underpinning virtues as the masses rush to a shadow of that which they feel profound shame to have overlooked in the time before the virus, and major exhibition centres (more ashamed still) battle it out, auction and fisticuffs, for the right to host the last, lost, Liberated. My better self, enacted elsewhere, afforded by all of this an easier life of Brüt Imperial, Marron Glacé and Walker's Sensations (even when they aren't on promotion). But for now? Film is (still!) the liberating application in the margins in search of a proper world... and never the twain shall meet.

An uncertain upload window makes its case behind this Word document. Behind that there is a smattering of unfinished document tabs insolent over Léon Comerre's *The Flood of Noah and His Companions*, and a foot beyond that there are double-glazed windows with a few notes stickied over, and then a grass against cutting, and then a tree bearing blossom (to which I return often to check that it really does smell like marzipan), with cousin chump and a short axe beneath the branches and yesterday's empty Guinness can the airgun couldn't puncture (we missed) set back by a foot; behind this, upwards, the Malvern hills and the sun of many days behind it all. It's not dark yet but it's getting there.*

* Before you mistake me for one in bed with the much-derided French authors summer-housing the lockdown as 'sleeping beauties,' know for what it's worth that I have permanently lost my home as a consequence of this and have only a bunk in this Midlands bolt hole as meaningful support.

A virus has presented itself, said to be long overdue in its coming. Said to be just the beginning. All over, those who aren't obviously sick or dying from the virus avoid each other in novel and militarily enforced ways. Only an hour ago outside the local Co-op a woman pressed her (masked) nose against the wall to avoid my passing her, thoughtless: we were less than two metres apart. After a closure that sent shockwaves through the local community, the chip shop has reopened: enthusiasts in their 'normal' clothes now punctuated by Mad Max sweatshop accessories, wait more keenly even than at airport departure gates. I expect the virus' legacy in terms of the queue to be positive: its authority undone by the gaps as necessity or hangover. And on-air travel too, which everyone seems too scared to declare a luxury which ought to be banned for businessmen, investors, and especially for tourists; a luxury which everybody knows by its very nature—climate apocalypse or no climate apocalypse—is confusing and wrong. The Chinese takeaway remains closed 'for the foreseeable future due to an ingredient shortage.' The local NHS pharmacist's window is armoured with a wall of exorbitantly priced industrial-size and strength alcoholic concentration and painkillers. Here, in Worcestershire, the infection rate was 124th highest in the UK the last time I checked, compared to Hackney (where I came from) which takes second after Newham, rife. With screens and frames before me and with gates and doors to block out the hysteria and the nonchalance, I am blessed in a way that we say we are blessed and affect gratitude but never really get until it's gone (Howard Marks last night on *Banged Up Abroad*—the last refuge of cinematographic integrity on UK television—said you can't appreciate freedom until you've been freed). By telephone, by text, by email and in the media, all talk contorts itself around 'nothing will ever be the same again.' Rubbish, if the past is anything to go by, but for the sake of argument if nothing was the same again: according to who and what? I am one of many people copied into an email from one of Britain's great catalysts early on in the time of the virus—perhaps too early on—volunteering that this is the moment we exploit to take shape of a genuinely collective, self-sufficient and sustainable future, pooling our resources together 'to maximise and formalise mutual support, sharing costs to reduce any double spending but also to create.' It was an exciting response measured by its calm, clarity and anti-pessimism. Feedback trickled in but barely, which surprised me for the calibre and otherwise

breathless enthusiasm of so many copied into the prompt forward. A few well-meaning but lacklustre responses were made
(your footprints on the ceiling of the Chelsea Hotel *baby*, *et
cetera*), before the chain became a random and predictable shoot
'em up of links to lists of films, articles... content which would
at a push find dialogue with the possible emergent reality but
was at its core a tribute to the passing of time. And what a pity!
For here in the time of the virus was, for those of us fortunate
enough to have lost any false sense of security and fortunate
enough not to be suffering from the virus or responsible for
anyone who is (or deflecting self-importantly via bullshit jobs:
think-tanks; fashion magazines; film festival arbiters of nothing
OR doing real jobs like REFUSE WORKERS; we say yodel for
them every Friday at 8pm! And COURIERS; have whole milk
and a banana loaf ready AT ALL TIMES to respond as we should
to the patter of tiny feet on the path and the slap on the step
of your new libertarian socialist tome: heroes!) time literally
freed: it might want to kill you, but it wants to kill capital too.
Be it the garden of earthly delights before you, or behind closed
eyes-doors: however conditional, the time of the virus is a gift
as extraordinary as our making. Time to learn Italian (hell, why
not Welsh too?); Time to toss the marbles and build the bench;
to write the poem; to live, though confined, away for a while
from the trappings, and to work on a way permanently out of
them (because Goddess knows they'll make us pay in time).
To sign out and switch it off.

In the Douglas Sirk film *All That Heaven Allows*, Jane Wyman's Cary is pestered by a salesman, her children, and her best friend to get a television. *'All you have to do is turn that dial, and you have all the company you want, right there on the screen. Drama, comedy... life's parade at your fingertips.'* The young widow is pressured to refuse another go at love by the fear around her. Why upset those closest and why make yourself vulnerable when the great unifier of the screen is 'at your fingertips'? Ron (Rock Hudson) is the hunky, working class boy who sees the liberated potential in Cary. A viewing of *Heaven Allows* in the time of the virus suggests that Ron is the promise of the wild and the unknown to free time, not in fact an individual in pursuit of Cary, but already a part of her deepest and most possible self. She is falling in love with life, perhaps for the first time. Her motion to surrender at the end of the film is the final cull of the bad fantasy as it is imposed upon her (and us), as she (and as we) instead falls into the dark lavender fold of Ron's embrace; a blind leap into the unknown at the expense of all previously thought real.

'*Real isn't how you are made,*' said the Skin Horse. '*It's a thing that happens to you. When a child loves you for a long, long time, not just to play with, but* REALLY *loves you, then you become Real.*'

Ping! My interruption interrupted: another email through with a link to great content suddenly 'freed' online... and I see a pattern emerging. I see individuals and organisations desperate to retain their pitch in the field; desperate to harvest the feedback they're used to receiving when all is 'up and running'; to forecast our emergence from the time of the virus by blocking our emergence with timecoded assaults in all of their flash and their flesh and their colour AND SO with gusto UP my cursor leaps to the x in the left-hand corner of an already uncertain upload window (which was, in case it isn't obvious, a window prepped for the Liberated Film Club to find an online outlet). The deluge of unfinished somethings underneath is properly revealed, and everything feels a little freer, a little more present; the marzipan blossom, the Guinness, the hills and what is left of the light, and hail victorious to them. No! to adding to the slurry of links, articles, lists obscuring further the route ahead; No! to playing to the virus in the way that so many rightfully scared and already exhausted institutions and organisations do. 'Yes!' to asserting power over the drab fantasy of 'real' life, with a cautious appreciation for what it can do for us in its suspension at least and fingers x'd *destruction* of present time as we knew it. I don't imagine Liberated Film Club attendees would recognise what we posthumously call 'normal' as a reality worth resuming, and it is for those people, honouring their attendance and their individual participations, rather than spectatorships, that we stand apart from the human-centipede, blind in service to the consolidation of power gleaned from patronising the 'connectivity' co-opted by the screen 'at your fingertips.' Obviously, nothing can begin to approximate let alone be equivalent to the adventure and the risk of the thousand-fingered surface. Cinemas, cafes, bars. Even churches. I've printed for reference the statue by Francesco Quierolo in the Church of St Severus in Naples. Stay with me—look it up. Without the need to return to the computer to look at Quierolo's masterpiece, I've whittled my online activities down to a rare fix of my old misery crutch in amateur scuba videos... caving only occasionally to the more conventionally dynamic river-deep scavenging videos, and never further. Those people who I had invited to present future editions of the Liberated Film Club: perhaps I will ask from them what they cannot share? It isn't too late for everyone else (meaning YOU, please!) to send in a favourite image of fire.

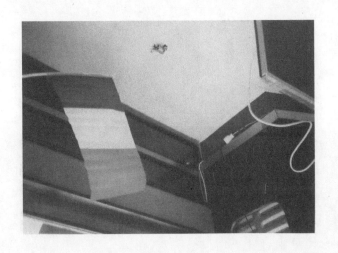

In spite of my resolve to sign out and switch it off, I do sometimes fall into the diary to see what *would have* been happening. In London an exhibition on the furniture of Casa Malaparte was due to open. Casa Malaparte (or Casa come me / House like me as its creator called it), in Capri, is best known as one of the main characters in Godard's *Contempt*. Conceived, built and lived in by Curzio Malaparte, a writer, filmmaker, and just about everything else whose life is the fiction to which ours should aspire, he designed the fireplace so that the ocean could be seen through the flames.

'He gazed at me with a serious expression and smiled. He told me that his two children, who were already in bed, had been overcome with a terrific fear during the first bombings, that the health of the youngest one had been seriously affected—and that he had evolved a means of changing the fearful bombings of Naples into an entertainment for his children. As soon as the alarm hooted through the night, my friend and his wife jumped out of bed and, gathering the two little ones in their arms began shouting merrily: 'What fun! What fun! The British planes are coming to throw their presents to you!' They went down into their cellar that offered scant and ineffectual shelter and, huddling there, they passed the hours of terror and death laughing and shouting, 'What fun!' until the boys fell happily asleep dreaming about the presents from the British flyers. From time to time, as the crash of the bombs and the crumbling of buildings came nearer, the little ones awoke, and the father said: 'Now, now, they are throwing down your presents!' The two boys clapped their hands with joy, shouting: 'I want a doll! I want a sword! Daddy, do you think that the British will bring me a little boat?' Toward dawn, when the hum of the motors moved off fading slowly into a sky that was already clear, the father and mother led the children by their hands into the garden, saying, 'Look for them, look! They must have dropped them on the grass.' The two boys searched among the rose bushes, wet with dew, among the lettuce plants and the tomato stalks, and they found a doll here, a little wooden horse there and, farther off, a bag of candy. The two children were no longer afraid of bombings, instead they waited anxiously for them and welcomed them joyfully.'**

**Curzio Malaparte, tr. C. Foligno, 'The Glass Eye,' *Kaputt* (London: Alvin Redman, 1948), pp.246–247.

To open, slit here

To open, slit here

★

Sender's name and address
Please show postcode

ALL THE KING'S HORSES

97 SCLATER STREET

LONDON

Postcode E1 6 HR

An airletter should not contain any enclosure

NOW THEN (MMXX)

At the time of the Club's death there were outstanding invitations to introduce; these were recovered in-part by the prompt contemplated in the curator's letter (preceding).

You've been asked to introduce a film screening that cannot and will not take place. It is for a cine-club that has ceased to exist. The films that will not be screened will remain unknown, even to those who may have appeared to view them.

At this screening that cannot and shall not take place, the film that would have been shown unspools within each film-goer, each filmgoer that cannot arrive, early or late, to take in the light's obsessive ironing of the supplicating screen.

In this cinema that does not exist, except in the non-memory of the blinking eyes that weren't there to see it, images spill forth: crawling clouds, fronds, scythes, hands hypnotically weaving in arcs of radiant toil. An interval cleaves, days suture. Cigarette smoke propelled only by the torpid luxury of cinematic time wends from open mouths. A door is left swinging. Waiting coagulates in this abandoned netherland, accumulates a thickly growing moss. Sinuous faces carved with lust beseech in their look offscreen towards an absent, unrequited lover. Dust motes pierce through the thickening gel of a pellucid glaze and inter-mittent flicker, floating in the projector's beam. The spectators who are not there cannot grow drowsy in the darkened warmth, sinking into their clotted limbs, melted by a sticky sun, the screen's ministrating gleam.

This non-existent film that is not shown and cannot be screened cannot be peeled away from its condensation into the sleepers' labial murmurations as they tussle and flow with the images, in waves. In this impossible film, at which these un-known slumberers cannot be in the theatre dormant, dreaming, cannot then jostle through the pillowing blur of crowds, the in-censed haze of processions and rituals of collective joy that run through the glassy apertures of the skull, like fissive slides.

What is that border between that film, which has not yet taken place, and that unbidden spectator who has not yet seen it, has not yet dreamt of an elsewhere of a thrumming life, where their exhausted, asthenic body becomes many

becomes an insurrectionary organism

becomes the sweat that dancers drip off in the leather bar of the mind

becomes the songs of *saudade* that an anti-army of lovers sing, locking arms, lubricated by bourbon, animated by fury, tears, rage becomes the marching amatory breathing of many throats and lungs in syncopating rhythms on the streets below the magnates' beaches

of striking not yet struck and struck one hundred, one thousand, one hundred thousand times, holding the line, poised to summon the voices of the dead?

What can't be shared can't be spared the negation of appearing.

What lingers, irreducible: a daydream of another, as yet unlived, time that will rip open the screen.

A couple of years ago I offered to contribute a bit of time, support, and film know-how to a group of Jewish socialists who were putting together a no-budget documentary on a complex topic, and who had little experience of documentary production or distribution. In the first instance the documentary was to show the mechanisms by which a Black Jewish woman, a socialist, had been targeted by a right-wing fringe group, whose attack was amplified by protagonists in the mainstream, resulting in her being portrayed throughout the media as an antisemite. This case study was to open broader questions about the political and media climate in Britain and to challenge a hegemonic narrative that had taken hold.

For those who are unfamiliar with how this works, a typical method used by contemporary anti-socialist militants involves trawling through an individual's social media accounts, sometimes going back years, taking fragments of a conversation from their context, then attributing to them the worst possible interpretation, and finally, paraphrasing the author's words in line with their negative reading. This is then put out in a press release, whereupon it is repeated across media reports and outraged public commentary, in endless iterations. The original claim is never subjected to critical scrutiny, despite the frequent availability of alternative interpretations, or often, of material evidence of blatant misrepresentation. Organisations that are marginal and patently partisan are treated unquestioningly as reliable sources of information.

Sometimes meetings of socialists are secretly recorded and a similar operation takes place, involving the extraction of phrases that can be presented after the fact to shine a negative light on the speaker. No matter if the speaker is herself Jewish. Such materials can be archived for months or years, and then released with further, similar materials at an opportune moment, providing a cumulative effect. Public shunning, shaming and calls for other punishment inevitably follow.

Back to the film. What the film lacked in craft skills, it made up for through its argument, and in the compelling testimonies of its expert witnesses.

The launch of the film took place at the Rio Cinema in Hackney, under tight security that was paid for by the group of Jewish socialists. This precaution was taken in light of physical threats against the subject of the film, and a history of aggressive disruption of events by activists hostile to anti-Zionist Jews.

Most concerning of all, a previous attempt to screen an early draft of the film at a community centre had had to be abandoned 15 minutes into the screening, after a bomb-threat resulted in the entire building being evacuated.

Fortunately, on this occasion the screening and panel discussion, which was also live-streamed to two cinemas in other cities, went off successfully and the full-to-capacity audience was engaged and animated. Several well-known film directors who were in attendance committed to officially endorse the film. An MP who showed up told the organisers he thought it was an important film that deserved a wider audience, and he promised he would try to book a room for a screening and discussion at the House of Commons in two weeks' time.

The following week, one of my colleagues received a text message saying that in a closed meeting of MPs, someone had expressed outrage because she'd discovered that a room had been booked for a screening of the documentary. The MP said she didn't know who was behind the booking, but she'd 'find out'. Other MPs joined in the outrage, shouting 'SHAME!' and hissing sarcastic remarks. The atmosphere had been 'monstrous,' the text message had said.

The next morning, I woke to the BBC radio news announcing calls for the MP to resign. By nine in the morning, a video recording had been leaked to the press that showed the MP speaking at a meeting one year previously. A section of his speech was presented to suggest that he was saying something that was more or less the opposite of what he had actually said. He issued a clarification and an apology at midday but was suspended anyway by 5pm.

The screening and discussion at the House of Commons was not to be. A newspaper article quoted an outraged MP describing the film (which she had not seen) as 'offensive' and claiming that it broadcast the 'hate-filled rhetoric' of its much-vilified subject.

Meanwhile in Nottingham, a local branch of the same Jewish group had decided to hire an auditorium at an arthouse cinema. However, the manager called to inform the group that they could not use the premises for the screening after all. The manager cited 'a risk of the threat of violence' and cancelled the booking. A letter of complaint was sent to the cinema, and an alternative venue found.

Despite these setbacks, the film successfully toured around the UK through grassroots networks, often to small-scale or informal venues, playing to interested audiences who wanted to discuss the issues it raised, sometimes presumably in order to make sense of the gap between their own experience as socialists and what they were hearing in the press week after week.

By this point, having helped set-up a mechanism to manage screening requests and distribution arrangements via a website, my involvement with the project came to an end.

*

Retrospectively, this troubling drama seems impossible to narrate in singular terms. Understanding the context involves recognising the convergence of different interest groups who promoted a narrative while studiously ignoring readily available information that contradicted it.

This cannot only have been about stigmatising critics of Israel and of Zionism, though this is certainly an important component. What can explain the investment of so many non-Jews on the right and on the centre-left of the establishment, many of whom had previously promoted dehumanising narratives about immigrants, Muslims and others, now saying they are very exercised about 'antisemitism-on-the-left'? And why was this group, that included politicians, newspaper editors, celebrities and commentators, simultaneously entirely uninterested in, and dismissive of the experiences of critical Jewish socialists, such as my friends?

Writer and activist Barnaby Raine speaking on this topic recently, asks what the moral panic about 'antisemitism-on-the-left' is really about if it is not about Jews.

Raine suggests that Jews are being instrumentalised in particular ways. On the one hand the Jew abroad is re-imagined in terms of a macho, muscular Zionism, the pioneer settler 'expanding the frontiers of Europe'; and on the other, the Jew at home in Britain is imagined as a vulnerable figure, in need of protection from barbarous hordes of Palestinians, Muslim immigrants and their gullible allies on the left. To these people then, Jews serve as an alibi for white society. Those who are worried about the anger and demands of formerly colonised peoples cast themselves as protectors of Jews. The figure of the Jew becomes a pretext for anti-Muslim, anti-immigrant feeling

—in the way that the protection of white women from the supposed violence of black men, has been constructed as a pretext for anti-Black racists.

So, what does this moral panic conceal, and why has it emerged now? Raine points to a profound anxiety about the end of neoliberal technocracy following the financial crash of 2008, that has seen the return of class politics and the return of a politics of confrontation. This appears to have taken an entire political establishment, that had come to believe in the declaration of the triumph of capitalism following the fall of the Berlin wall, as 'the end of history,' by surprise.

Soon, politicians and media commentators on the right and the centre-left were suggesting that anti-capitalism and anti-elitism are somehow intrinsically linked to antisemitism. This seems not only to crudely misread the structural (and impersonal) basis of actual critiques of capitalism, but it also internalises and reproduces antisemitic tropes that imagine Jews to be embodiments of wealth and capital. Nevermind that, throughout the 20th century, the British establishment was not only profoundly antisemitic, but it took Jews to be synonymous with the supposed threat posed to capitalism by communism.

Here are just three examples of this confused contemporary thinking:

I   Labour MP Siobhain McDonagh said in a BBC interview in 2019, 'it's very much part of their politics, of hard-left politics, to be against capitalist [sic] and to see Jewish people as the financers of capital, ergo you are anti-Jewish people.' Interviewer: 'In other words to be anti-capitalist you have to be antisemitic'. McDonagh: 'Yes.'

II   In the *New Statesman* in 2018, Matt Bolton and Frederick Harry Pitts wrote about the 'deep-seated theoretical underpinnings of left critiques of capitalism that have antisemitism as their logical consequence.

III   The Board of Deputies of British Jews and the Jewish Leadership Council wrote an open letter to the Labour Party in 2018 that complained of 'a far-left worldview that is instinctively hostile to the mainstream Jewish communities [...] in which the mainstream Jewish communities are believed to be a hostile entity—a class enemy.'

Leaving aside the exclusionary conception of 'mainstream' Jewishness in the last quotation, the logic of the above theses implies that any form of anti-elitism, or challenge to class inequality, can potentially be construed as antisemitic. This is quite a claim coming at a time when inequalities have never been more extreme or more visible, when the far-right is on the ascent, and when managerial politics of the past 40 years that oversaw the financial crash, has shown itself to be incapable of responding to most of the pressing crises we face.

*

In the long history of anti-communism, the hunt for Reds has always taken on the conspiratorial and authoritarian characteristics ascribed to communism. Today, there is no revolutionary communist threat, yet a certain anti-communist fervour appears to be stalking official public discourse, while the right rises and rises.

Official figures show that 0.08% of the UK Labour party's 540,000 strong membership were subject to allegations of antisemitism in the period 2018–19. Investigations have been launched against at least 25 members who are themselves Jewish, which suggests that Jewish party members are disproportionately exposed to being investigated for antisemitism. In all cases, those accused are not permitted to know the identity of their accusers or the specific charge against which they need to defend themselves and are forbidden to talk to anyone else about the investigation, even relatives or lawyers, at the risk of facing yet more disciplinary charges.

One can only imagine the emotional and psychological toll this has taken on those who have been caught up in a factional war, through the actions of third parties with a political axe to grind. In case it needs saying, there is a long and dark history of Jews being used as proxies in a political power struggle.

Were my friends naive to hope that cinema had the power to create a fissure in a monolithic media narrative that had denied their voice and their experience as left-wing Jews?

At the very least one might say that reaction to the mere existence of such a film successfully demonstrated the underlying hypocrisy, intolerance and institutional capture of those liberal critics who regularly accuse the left of Stalinism, abuse and underhandedness. These critics apparently feel justified in

deploying those very tactics in order to neutralise the threat they
see in those on the left calling for radical change in the form
of economic, racial and climate justice.

Two domestic VHS videotapes, hand labelled. One made in 1987, possibly '88. The other, 1993.

Let's call them Tape 1 and Tape 2.

I remember four scenes from Tape 1.

(1)

Random switching between TV channels, scratch video style.
It looks like 1990s MTV made by someone who only read about
it. Rapid cuts, attempting to evoke a feeling of media overload,
but limited by a choice of only four stations and a sluggish re-
mote control. The sequence is shot off the screen. The edges
of the image curve backwards from the convex centre of the
glass. You can see phasing lines and patches textured by finger
smears or static that's not been wiped away. Dark areas on the
screen show the reflection of the camera. The soundtrack is a
song by The Art of Noise. I forget which, but it involves clever
arrangements of sampled voices and crisp Fairlight synths.
It's dubbed from a vinyl LP, which accounts for tiny pops and
crackles on the audio. At one point, the image switches to a live
broadcast of a Gilbert & Sullivan opera. I remember it being *The
Mikado*, but I could be wrong. A group of actors dressed in red
robes and ornate head gear is sat holding court. The Art of Noise
song hovers quiet and sparse, then suddenly bursts into the
sound of a large choir. A heavenly epiphany. Right on the beat,
by chance, the actors all stand and turn to look stage left.

(2)

Interior, night. A locked-off, low-angle shot of an upright piano.
The outer casing of the instrument has been removed to show
the hammers and strings. A spider plant is perched on top of
a narrow stand made from carved bamboo. The plant is lit from
below, throwing the shadows of its leaves across the piano and
the wall behind. The corner of a window hung with Venetian
blinds can be seen to the right of the composition. The vibe is
Casablanca. Or 80s *noir* revival. Or French bistro. The scene
aspires to have jazz music and a spinning ceiling fan but has
neither. Instead, the scene is suffused with a reverb-like ambi-
ence, which is made by keeping the piano's loud pedal pressed,
allowing the strings to resonate with vibrations inside the room
and passing traffic on the road outside. The shot is held still
for some time. At one point, the shadow of a small figure wearing a Panama hat falls across the scene.

(3)

Handheld. The inside of a dark, cluttered garden shed. There
are cobwebs on the window and the shed looks as if it's been
grown rather than built. The door opens, and the camera rushes
outside, swinging wildly. It speeds along a concrete path that
runs next to a narrow lawn. It wants to be played back at a faster
speed, manic, like film shot at ten or twelve frames per second,
but can't be, so it relies on the running and flailing camera to
convey a sense of energy. The light suggests an overcast summer
day. Thick, muggy air before a thunderstorm. A cheerful, thrashy
guitar song plays.

(4)

Video feedback, long and boring. A tunnel-effect achieved
by plugging a camera into the TV and pointing the lens at the
screen. Video of video.

Tape 2 has a cardboard slipcase carefully covered in pale green marble pattern paper, and is labelled on the front in Letraset, Old English Blackletter style.

Only two short images from this tape come to mind:

(A)

A colourful abstract composition, like a detail from a large expressionist canvas, but mutating in slow, jerky motion. It's rendered in blues, yellows and greens, hyped vivid by a basic digital 'paint' effect. Think: *Ashes to Ashes*. The image is accompanied by the Polygon Window track *Quino-Phec*. A gentle, ambient piece that sounds aerated and distant, like the noise from a fairground that's drifted some miles across open fields.

(B)

The famous black-and-white clip of scientist J. Robert Oppenheimer, filmed in 1965, describing his feelings following the detonation of the Trinity nuclear bomb test in New Mexico, 1945. He quotes from the *Bhagavad Gita*: 'Now I am become death, the destroyer of worlds. I suppose we all thought that, one way or another.' The clip repeats, and each time the quality of the image degrades. The details thicken out into high contrast areas of pattern, the effect of a tape being copied, then copied again from the copy.

I was twelve when I made Tape 1. Seventeen when I did Tape 2. I made both using video cameras my Dad brought home from work. He taught at a comprehensive school on the edge of Oxford and had procured the cameras second-hand for use with the vocational studies pupils he taught. The cameras lived in his office, coming home with him for 'safe keeping' at weekends and during the holidays. It was really just an excuse for us to play with them. Tape 1 was made using a 1979 Ferguson Videostar. A bulky trigger-grip camera connected via a long thick cable to a separate silver VCR unit about the size of a large shoebox. Small control buttons and hefty DIN sockets ran along the front end, and a VHS tape could be loaded in via a cradle that opened on top of the box. The VCR came in a black leather satchel with a carrying strap, powered by a heavy battery brick. I was a small 12-year-old. When slung across my shoulder, the unit hung down to my knees.

I was then a devout pupil of the Argos catalogue, whose digital watch, portable keyboard and camera pages I pored over. I believed that staring at them long enough would manifest this unattainable technology in my life. Argos told me that you could get all-in-one camcorders that were lightweight and sat on your shoulder. The clunky Videostar was clearly obsolete, but that didn't bother me. The camera and a blank VHS tape represented pure potential, the same way a freshly sharpened pencil and brand-new sketchbook did.

A few years later Dad upgraded the school camera to a JVC camcorder, which felt like the future after working with the Videostar. It had built-in digital effects, but audio dubbing still had to be done using the onboard mic pushed up close to a speaker. I used this for Tape 2. By my late teens I had an idea that something called experimental film existed. I'd read about it in books but had not seen any besides the occasional Derek Jarman or Peter Greenaway film shown on TV late at night. I was probably more interested in music videos but didn't make much of a distinction in artistic value between an art house film and a pop promo: it was all new to me, all of interest. I had an idea that I might want to go to art school, and Tape 2 was made with that aspiration in mind. Mum had bought me a blank VHS tape for this express purpose, which we kept in the chest of drawers that the TV stood on.

Tape 1 was made intuitively. Before the Videostar first came home in Dad's Lada, I'd been messing around with blank audio cassette tapes, making cut-up sound collages from snippets of records. I had a combination tape and record player. I'd set a cassette up to record with the pause button pressed, find the part of the record I wanted—usually a lyric I liked—then drop the needle and release the pause, quickly pressing it again once I'd caught the sample. Often there would be mistakes, and tape artefacts, such as clicks and squelching noises which I discovered I liked the sound of. I didn't understand them to be tape experiments, because I was not aware that I was experimenting. I simply enjoyed recombining sound and words, especially if it made me laugh, if it tickled my love of nonsense. The sources I used weren't cool. They included Cliff Richard and the Young Ones' Comic Relief charity version of *Living Doll*, and Paul Hardcastle's theme tune to *Top of the Pops*. I remember a BBC sound effects record too, and the incidental music to *Doctor Who*. I knew about The Art of Noise—I found them funny—and there was likely a Pet Shop Boys song in the mix too, as I was deeply into them at the time. I remember using a single by the group Red Box, then popular and now completely forgotten. Those pop records were more sophisticated, but to me at the time, *West End Girls* and BBC *Comedy Sound Effects Vol. 4* were of equal merit. I had one foot still firmly in childhood, as the other tentatively crossed into adolescence.

The channel-switching sequence on Tape 1 was based on a similar principle to the audio cassettes. I enjoyed the random juxtapositions of images, heightened further by chance moments of synchronicity between music and picture when I dubbed a song over the top. The Videostar could not take a feed directly from the TV, so I had to shoot the screen and flip the channels manually, but not fast enough to create the strobing effect I wanted. I know I had seen fast, choppy editing on *Network 7*, a youth TV show being broadcast at Sunday lunchtimes on Channel Four that year, and something similar on the BBC music show *Snub TV*. I was likely trying to imitate these, even if I didn't quite understand what the editing styles signified.

I discovered the video feedback effect by accident, spinning around the living room with the camera, delighting in the blurry, dizzying ghost trails that the VHS made. The tunnelling-effect looked just like the opening credits of *Doctor Who*, which was then my favourite TV show. The locked-off shot of the piano was an attempt to recreate the atmosphere of Browns, a French-style bistro chain I had been taken to for a birthday treat, and which

I believed to be the epitome of adult sophistication. They served thin-cut chips—the menu called them fries—and coffee with froth on it. There were palm leaves, wood floors, jazz music and waiters wearing little black aprons and white shirts. Half of them were my Dad's school pupils working their Saturday jobs. I was the shadowy figure in a Panama, a hat taken from my dressing-up box. The thrashy song that accompanied the garden shed scene was a song called *Slipper Dog*, recorded during a school concert by The Jennifers, a band I was playing in at the time.

From speaking to other artists and musicians over the years, I've learned that I was far from unique in finding ways to intuitively mess with consumer electronics. I long to see the tapes again. But Tape 2 was lost around the time I left for art school and Tape 1 erased at some point during my teenage years. Either it became an embarrassment to me, or I urgently needed to tape a film off the TV and decided to sacrifice it for something that today I could find in five seconds on my phone. *Taxi Driver*, *The Shining*, or some other drearily common classic.

It's been almost thirty years since I last watched those videos. I can't be sure that the narrative I have constructed of my creative development would be corroborated by what was on the tapes. A few VHS cassettes still hide in the back of the chest of drawers beneath the TV at my parents' house. Occasionally, on visits home, I look in the hope that either tape has magically reappeared. No luck as yet.

An affective representation of feeling
the architecture of our dwellings
grown very familiar and detailed
a longing to be a receptor to the energetic emanations of others.

CODA

I Am A Film
Stephen Watts

I am a film
The forest of red spruce is burning inside me
The gold of my intestines is a frozen lake of rain
The tree in my eye is a thousand years old
I am a film. The skins
Of my dream are forty-five buffalo hides
The urinal of heaven is resin burnt to dust.

I am a film.
A black line of nomads on a march of winter snow
A vestige of nightmare in the core of a mountain ash
A collapsed sheep fed apricots above the tree line
The mobility of resin in sleets of blood-berry time
The pulsing of blood in ancestor's shadows

I am a film. I am a shroud
Over the face of a girl cornered by monotony.
I am a shroud placed by the art of political morons.
I am the flimsy space where breath can't decay.
I am the way where there never was a way.
I am a film.

I am the ewe's milk sold from the shack
The cheeses of despair out in the vodka ruts
The archives left out on the rooves to dry
The persistence to choose without knowing why
The words that form in the slick of the liver
The antonym of trauma in the road-edge hut
This is language that forms in the gut
I am a film.

I am Rumi who climbs in my un-windowed wall
I am Rilke who meets me up the deep stairwell
I'm Marina who gazes through my shut-eyed eye
I'm Jibanananda tossed high by a car out of hell
I'm Cesar Vallejo in some burnt mestizo cell
I'm Chairil Anwar in the highest high-rise
I'm despair on despair that climbers despise
I am a film.

I'm the sun seen through the belly of a horse
I'm a foal un-foaled by the red mare's nurse
I'm a raft in the rapids, a curse in the floods
I am vodka urns drunk down incessant muds
I'm the moon that falls in the deep tureen
I'm the mean of meaning, the meaning
Of mean, the algebra of language.
I am a film.

The gabbeh of colour & the gabbeh of dream
Five little children in a meadow of poppies
A class-full of goats in a blue tent's screen
Five little children who wake up & scream
Forty-five gabbehs laid to dry by a torrent
Rags of colour tied to the trees
I am a film.

I am gorse that burns in the coconut air
Coma crests of storm that march on the moor
Shark's teeth of islands across a burnt-out sea
Displaced peasants beneath a monopoly flag
Legion on legion of exiled contadini
Paths to the shielings that run into bog-weed
Scratches of song from a muted tongue
I am a film.

Four-billion-year-old mountains seen from a plane
A shepherd's language shared by fifteen men
A whole earth held in a spun pool of water
A vagina betrayed by a single red garter
This is language climbing from the aorta
I am a film.

A cone of wood for the making of charcoal
Smoke rising straight from an emptied village
Season on seizure in an unfinished ritual
Thunder walls on an epic snow journey
One warm commitment that is never enough
I am a film.

Children. A necklace
From a war yet to come.
Fragments. Scoriae. A rebuilt city.
Ten thousand incomprehensible avenues.
In the midst of this rehearsed world
That only stuns with its affluence.
Naturally we rejected the scars of
A disremembered time.
Memory that seeks out its scars.
As if its bricks were bruised off air.
As if the tenderest child were to
Shed her own dear life.
As if the Hanging Gardens were
No longer hanging in green time.
All the protesting nonsense of
Intricate days burnt down to nothing.
I am a film.

Such pure faces, such masked
Energies, such perverse visions.
O angel
Smile in the foetus of the world
O smile of angels here in our now.
Komitas the mad never made a film
But nor did he not ever make a film.
His whole unwayward life was one
Unwavering commitment of film,
A reel that ....

....

Or when you put your eye
So close up to a flower you can
No longer make out what it is
But a blur of blue and shape.
But its filaments, its stamen
Are still there, miraculous
Growths of what can only be.
Extraordinary world patterns :
That from which we were made.
Or like a chapel in the mountains
Rorsached with winter snows.
Or like the astonishing vortex of
Crepe that a mouse makes her nest
From, as complex as any
Mathematical structure of our earth,
Worked only by instinct & trust.
Such nests I preserved in my home
Until they were burnt accidentally
In the cold winters of regeneration.

Film is prosaic poetry only
Because poetry is essentially
Prosaic : what is quotidian still is
The stuff of our daily bread.
Pasolini knew that : but who
Knows Pasolini in these days.
In these days of autism & bliss.
Who knows the urge of his rabbia
The contexts of his urgent rage
Though we occupy glutton cities
And try to energise new options.
Pasolini knew poetry is work.

Film, I tell you, is the most urgent & radical prosaic.
Film is pure poetry in our beautifully impure world.
Whirl of pattern in the innermost whorl of our brain.
Vagrant tongues that curl meanings through walls.
Women who can penetrate any wall without holes.
Women who can breach any peace that betrays us.
Zigzag of curdled energy in a rented meeting house.
Sheets of dark snows approaching over the moors.
Garbled language in bitter-tight coils of our world.
Savage snowstorm in such lamentable mountains.

Film, I tell you, is the most urgent & radical prosaic.

Old woman living life yearlong in a raw baita.
Her slowness vital yeast for our possible future.
Markets of pomegranate & peppers in thick rain.
Futures mercantiled for blubber in great cities.
Cynicisms choked back in bad-summer lattes.
....
Film, I tell you is the most urgent prosaic
I am a film.

It was siege warfare
They ate the leaves off the trees.
White wolves surrounded the houses.
All the villages & towns about razed.
Severed heads held aloft by masked men.
Absolute worlds of understanding never
Meeting political ethics of raw fratricide.
City of the sun splayed out in red deserts.
Calm boulevards reduced to dirt rubbles.
Little children screaming at their friends.
We who yearn the lyric calm of courage.
We who learn to cynic cornered outrage.
We who charmed the birds down from
The trees. I am my own language.
My language is me.
I am a film.

When I bypassed the city in the desert.
When I bypassed the hatreds in the senate.
When I gabbled at the air in my intestines.
When I garbled what matters in investing.
When I fluked the selfie of some murder.
When I puked the surfeit of my masters.
When I said all of poetry's cunning labour.
When the city I'd bypassed self-exploded
With the motive for its being unrecorded.
Sun-city that's exploding in the morning.
Two different worlds of understanding.
White city of the sun !
I am a film.

(

Confirm Humanity
  or Traits Seen as Symptoms
  or Presently: Aspiring to an Eloquent Alarm
  or Long Fertile Collaborations
Gareth Evans

In Memory of—and for—Louis Benassi (1961–2020),
with Respect and Love for His Example

Complete basic training in how the world works, the remorseless
Working of things, strain before the box closes to black.
    —Fred Moten, from 'code and tone'

(Lucid flowing conversations)

You already know enough. So do I. It is not knowledge we lack.
What is missing is the courage to understand what we know and
to draw conclusions.
    —Sven Lindqvist, from *Exterminate All the Brutes*

In the enemy language it is necessary to lie.
    —Sean Bonney, from *Happiness, Poems After Rimbaud*

The END TIMES are back, if they ever weren't. The difference
with this round: they really might be what they've always
claimed.

At the four-way junction the lights are green and red all
over; how to cross, why, when. Two women swing a living child
between them. Overheard: 'wait for the green man... Ah, the
green man!' If only! Then there surely would be glad end-times,
as we enter the age of the *verdant* fuse and a cycle both vehicular
and seasonal, leaving at least the era of the electrical way behind
us in the rear-view mirror of the car that no longer will exist.

So many masks we wear (not in the bourgeois adultery novel mode but in the material over the face manner). Who do they
conceal? They're screens but nobody is changing behind them
in a flickered silent movie way, hanging stockings gauzed as
moth wings over the panels; rather they are ebbing and flowing
existentially, from crisis to collapse to a rallying posture. Why
aren't there more bank robberies now that coverings are a given?
Because the money isn't real anymore, that's why. How do you
hold up wiring? Or not even wiring—air...

When you do glimpse a visage on these streets, so many
(too many—your call) women here look like they're in 1960s
French New Wave films, while too many (so many—your...) men
look either like they're in British 90s TV, or they're Appalachian,
as if this was a mountain range in East London and not West
Virginia. They sprawl reading (books open on stumps like large
butterflies, briefly) on the sun's loved logs (the timber to text
loop closed at last) in small clusters as if they had just felled the
trunks and were squatting—safari style—on their target. Others

walk the long light across the common ground, inverse to those folks lining the Zócalo flagpole shadow in Francis Alÿs' Mexico City square.

They queue at garden centres. In this there is some initiative, however appropriated. We should have stolen soil, spaded it up at night from private enclaves and piles, lowering the earth density of the rich in places—the more to boost our own spirit level—just as their actions have seen the ocean rising in and over others.

The park today—populated to a degree that it is now a polis within the city—suggests nothing so much as the foundational sequence of Charles and Ray Eames' *Powers of Ten*, pulling out in equivalent retreats from its foundational supine limb to reach the whole of the known universe. In a palpably real sense this is the only film we ever need to watch because, by definition, it contains all others within it. There is literally nowhere else to go, to draw from, to be... Imagination, spirit and death: all are contained within it, and therefore all possible human ideas, expressions, artefacts... movies.

The people are here because spring is coming, and they are pitching early, festival-style, claiming their turf at the frontier of the cold. In wait they lie, mad for it, cabin-feverish, desperate to speak and spit their speech out IRL, to know and feel that other bodies exist as sweating machines, no longer only tactile in the head. The season is indeed changing. There is a new dynamic at play, porosity to the borders between light, shadow, blossom, smoke and mist. The tree shakes its flowers out and they hang in the afternoon like snow that stalled in the falling. Silently then, spring is opening its mouth in the soft blue copses—enigmatic, simple joy—but the question it surely is asking (aren't we all, constantly, consciously or in the deep late / early hour unsure of mental status): what is to be done?

Yes. *What* is to be done? What *is* to be done? What is to be *done*? Despair's refrain, its terraced chant: squirrels struggle with the rodents for the sweet, damp woodpile. That other man over there near the ivy trembles like his whippet. This shade-of-pale French bulldog fails to climb a bench. A single, soundless ice-cream van idles by the gates. There is a score of teens playing several games between them on forbidden AstroTurf. They scaled the high and crosshatched fence; hang there for a moment, before dropping, agile as asylum seekers, etching on the mind the wintry border post of *Eternity and a Day*.

An iceberg the size of greater London has calved—snapped off like the branch we're sitting on, has left Mother Antarctica to melt its massive waters into greater swells. The capital *is* the melting. *What is to be done?*

This was first an essay hinged around a lockdown, posited on pandemic. It mutated in the dying of the year through a great, shared loss and now, its face grooved by the wire, it tries to place itself in the yet to come, while knowing where we were, and somewhat where we started out. Since the local has become all we can be sure of, the door of the house we pace past daily has braided itself shut—ivy has taken the hinges and lock: is this a sign of wealth gone AWOL or of an absence very much unchosen?

Every dusk might be the last dusk, each dawn the one against which we measure our holding position until the next. What we use as way stones, mile stations in our passage through such quietly wild not knowing are—it seems to me—images from films. Make your own selection. Frame grabs, stills and sequences—to everyone their own, age and place and taste dependent—marking either threat or how much lost—images (not only motion, but still—sometimes the painting or a photograph) are how we try to hold onto what is happening or *not* happening.

With very few and well discussed, quite literal, literate exceptions, it is not fiction on the page that helps us here (we shall not dwell on music, in its glory, here, as it stands apart, a grail, ideal). A book suggests narrative progression in a way that pictorial selection—even from a classic motion picture spilling over with story—does not necessarily provide. And how can we claim a resolved telling, while we are in the midst, as everything is molten? The literary also advocates that the interior life, seedbed of the novel's long transmission, is somehow fit for purpose, focus, clear reception, when I doubt right now it is, doubt it very much.

Given this, it is only those writers whose trade is dark unsettlement, rupture, and the bitter consolation of the spaces in between, whose work is driven by the startling visual—for me it's the cinematic stylists soaked in *film as influence and exemplar* —who provide a guidance now, a viable map of the present atmospheric, a possible direction of travel. Out of paranoia and obsession to details of change they script lines of luminous precision, mysterious as light, it being the first and final.

However, and by definition, any and all of these are images we *know*, have read and taken in and so, in that way, pictures of the *defined*, however alien to us they might begin.

We turn our poor attention now to what we could not know...

(Lingering fecund collisions)

Let me remind you that everyone with a window already jumped.
   —Joshua Beckman, from *New Haven*

Nothing changes. The bones of the mammoths
are still in the earth.
   —Adrienne Rich, from *End of an Era*

You *had* to *be* there. Accept no substitutes except this volume
here. The black box of the auditorium *was*. How adequately
to celebrate the *place* of this purpose—without Close-Up Film
Centre, and its instinctive understanding of the project, all
of this would be as tears in rain, and perhaps not even that: all
movements need a site, a meeting ground, a common carpet,
a clearing; such generous permission makes the mission
tangible.

   The Liberated Film Club (henceforth LFC) is, therefore,
not only a room, but it does need one—to incarnate itself as
more than pure idea. And, once made available, this chamber
cannot be moved (or the project shift from there). It is not a
sealed interior space aspiring—like a pyramid tomb—to tran-
scend history. Rather, it is the sum of all its events and screenings, the lives and approaches of its audiences, the experiences
of its staff, the weather meteorological, social, political, economic of the world on which it rides, and the same applies to
the LFC itself, planted like a passing tree in the earth of this
conjunction (always *unsettling* to think of Francis Bacon's Reece
Mews palette pit being containered to Dublin—a simple glance
at the before / after will reveal the transgressive impossibility
of the intention; now the 'new' will overwrite the actual for all
who do not know and even challenge the memory for those who
did; better for it to be shipped into the flatland of the photograph alone).

   In a room with desirable strangers, know and not what
might be (so it is with us in life entire), but rarely ever in our
interactions: what will come, will come...

Perception is social, not merely personal.

Audience
           Attendance
                      Attention
                                &
A tension

*

The Aleph is an open door on blueprint plans for building: A, the ox head, the animal in the system, the Minotaur in the labyrinth who wants out as much as Ariadne does; A again. In Borges' story of the sign, the Aleph 'is a point in space that contains all other points. Anyone who gazes into it can see everything in the universe, every angle simultaneously, without distortion, overlapping, or confusion.'

Useful to us is this not (let's think Antonioni, poet of *the space* that, like the fade in music, persists and then persists regardless of us there or not, watching, listening, more— people are the blur at best—time lapse taking, the people fall away—still, the place endures).

So it begins: we have location, we have the project planned—tender, risky, vulnerable, almost like a wound *before* the blow. The LFC is cartographic, serving as it can the place described just now, while wishing population for its reason. It triangulates twice:

1. The experience of the people in the place described
2. Loss, memory, recovery—cinematic salvage from the plunging void

The mentioned tension is also formed of fear. We have a motivation, more than one: concern and its flipside, a rallying commitment, advocacy. These gather around the screen, of course. Here the known and not known mingle. It is not as simply managed as one being on each side: they're mongrel, they're promiscuous. The audience's not knowing is matched by protagonist Schtinter's own tall hesitation; how will the seated eyes react? It starts with the unknown but closes deeper in the mystery, fuelled by sheer attendance. These are films freed from the desire to be known: in this fact their liberating fuel.

We know *all too well* that the screen conceals as much as it reveals. The curtain around a hospital bed projects something that cannot be seen but which could hardly be described as hidden, the huge anxiety of the approaching relative. The world and the cinema are sudden relatives in intention, or at least production, currently. As ever and always, in this and all our considerations, the Möbius strip tells us what we need to understand.

Each time it is as if for the first time: that is LFC's irreducible proposal. What does it mean when all of it has already happened? We used to read, plan and schedule, book everything concerning holidays *in advance*, visit the sites, eat the meals on the page: the vacation itself was already redundant before it had occurred. In this way, LFC rips into the reality we have made much as a shark into a surfer's trailing leg. Prepare all you want, but you will never be able to prevent the bite, if the jaws want to close. The only way is *not to go at all*, in which case you have decided to remain alert but stop living.

So you sit down, you sit back. Your eyes are peeled, literally like fruit, for promise, revelation: their pulp is exposed to light and putrefaction, processes of being we know as terminal. The ride is all, a journey back to the source of what it means actually to see another world manifest 'in the same room'—the realm of saints, of miracle pavilions. Child wonder: short trousers in the primal wood, snap of branch, sudden call, the gloaming's damp and glisten.

*

Interior: two women stare into the opened mouth—darkness visible—of a lock-up garage. We cannot make out the contents or even the conditions. They stare, look at each other, stare again. We leave them still in transit. Is this cinema?

*

This is NOT about a *surprise* preview; a London Film Festival scratch 'n sniff ready meal. This is alchemical, proposing the never to be repeated transformation—transubstantiation even—of the hushed bond between speaker, audience and screen. Expanded cinema in this instance is no longer about multiple projections but about increasing the definitions of the possible. The LFC has the shape of an illuminated wall but the dimensions of the cosmos, because it contains all which can and might be—its darkness is as deep, its light as ancient and alive. It is the Eames machine rolled out across the schedule. And, like that work, the moment of immersion, the entry portal, could properly be found at any point.

Like the disappearing music—which has always played and continues to do so (we just visit it for a moment and one more)—so the films are running in a parallel portal called History or 'what was' and always will be. We're tuning in, picking up their rogue transmissions, as sweat-browed James Wood did the Blondie burn of *Videodrome*. We join them always mid- ...

and leave them as we found...

and so, incomplete, they are without a start or close, like those books that finish in the sentence—Kafka's *Castle*, Daumal's *Mount Analogue*—places like our own that know no final wall or definition, place, in short, that is a 'state' of mind. These films, however, also *start* inside a scene, regardless of the plot. That scene is our profound Anticipation, which must join the Aleph gang.

*

Exterior: a concrete yard: the broken vodka bottle holds the sun in several sharded pools. Is this cinema?

*

They're the motion pictures that can arm-wrestle the Black Square or the White into stilled submission. As infinite as each of these, but *temporally* ahead, they have dimensional advantage, and exist more in dialogue, if with any other wall-located work, with Lucio Fontana's slashed canvases, opening up a distance *back*, a rupture that makes more than just a 'work.' Closer they are to Yakuza full tattoos, Bradbury's *Illustrated Man*, the scene alive and changing with each breath, or glimpse or slump. Closer they are, these films, to the empty roads of lockdown, transports of delight now there is not a car in sight, and all is pure potential—every journey made, or that might be, within their silent lanes.

The LFC has prefaced this by pushing, more than any other practice, the portal in the ways described above. Remember *Two Lane Blacktop*, closing on a burning of the reel? Even there, the screen remained, a focus on the flames. At its core the LFC is not and never has been about the means. Its end is without end and far, far out beyond the threshold that we cross to access what it brings.

Such projection means the end of *fatigued* sleep, as the shared-screen dream of cinema becomes the common status of the soul: it's a screen for stopping the somnolence of shallow living, surface, fritter, all distraction.

*

Imagine an eye unruled by man-made laws of perspective, an eye unprejudiced by compositional logic, an eye which does not respond to the name of everything, but which must know each object encountered in life through an adventure of perception. How many colours are there in a field of grass to the crawling baby unaware of 'Green'—? How many rainbows can light create for the untutored eye? How aware of variations in heat waves can that eye be? Imagine a world alive with incomprehensible objects and shimmering with an endless variety of movement and innumerable gradations of color. Imagine a world before the 'beginning was the word.'
—Stan Brakhage, from *Metaphors on Vision*

*

Exterior: that man along the towpath, tall as tales, who dances like a tempest weathervane, yowling with a private keen delight to the headphone music that he so adores. He does not need the headphones to hear the sounds he hears. Is this cinema?

What happens after cinema happens?

Projecting engine of the entirely possible, the LFC understands that it provides a place within which one can reside, like music, clear of language. Burroughs called language a virus from outer space; we have our own earthbound variants well stocked, but the LFC situates its deep contamination elsewhere, inner space. It makes its own images there, finally of and for itself, never Abandoning Audience Attraction, but sufficient without it. Might it then be cousin to Trevor Paglen's picture-prolific machines, exchanging generated selfies inside their own vast circuits,

378

so far outside the human they might as well source from off-planet as secret visitations.

Where the LFC diverges *entirely* however from these A.I. proliferations—and please do kneel in praise with blessed thanks for *this*—is in its total lack of the two core components of our modern ruin: conflict and commodification. Yes, you might disagree on the quality of a chosen work with your viewing neighbour, but that is not our issue. There is a very real case to be heard that all images *made now* are *inherently* militarised: drone, game, data, deep fakes, news, revenge porn and much porn that isn't, that 'authored reality,' every dropped commercial, every party vid, every tracking shot over all that we have trashed...

The war is propaganda just for profit (buy the planes), the children on the dirt road playing are 'removed' from view for loading up an anti-aircraft strike ('they' claimed), the overcrowded boat that tips is out of site of land / help / mind. What is seen can be destroyed and what we see—or don't—can lead direct to damage.

The LFC is a campaign against the arms trade, is the opposite of a gun or an assault on the Capitol or a country because its image can't be bought, can't be 'used', does not circulate again, does not circulate for gain, often fights the power direct, and always stands against brute 'force' because what it shows is so clear of their radar that they stumble in its wake, unable to compute.

*

For the master's tools will never dismantle the master's house.
They may allow us temporarily to beat him at his own game, but
they will never enable us to bring about genuine change. And
this fact is only threatening to those women who still define the
master's house as their only source of support.
　　—Audre Lorde, from *The Master's Tools Will*
　　Never Dismantle the Master's House

*

Meanwhile, commodification works like Saint-Exupéry's python, swallowing a thing entire with its shape and digesting it into itself by draining purpose and then form, growing stronger on the deed. The radical uncertainty of the LFC resists this because it, as a target of predatory purchase, evades comprehension as a target. Like those soft creatures—why not call them deer—who can't deduce the tiger's orange bars, the system that would break us cannot stalk the LFC in all the background noise. Its camouflage is its *provisional* self. It also slips clear—while speaking so profoundly to the now—because of this uncertainty and lack of single fix, a photograph that remains a process, not a print. An image for our times, it could almost be the mainstream, hiding in plain sight. After all, what could be more radically uncertain than where and how we live, beset around with devils of *our* making, so many we have lost count, and all of whom will take us down, the only doubt being when (as if they can be held by calendars or clocks).

So, we live as always in an age of (not)-knowing:

1. Death but not how or when
2. Civilisational collapse but not how or when
3. What will come after but not how or when

The LFC does not resist this (not)-knowing but rather embraces it as the only way to be more fully present and attending (to the screening encounter and to its implications). That noted, it is not flippant or callous about real mortalities bought on by pandemic mal-provision and the huge grief attached to the terrible what-if of viral spread. Good unknowns feel rare right now.

Not to know can sometimes kill you, but not to know can also alleviate unnecessary concern and give what time remains a more complex and humane texture than it might otherwise possess, being directed as it likely could be towards a finally futile removal of what concerns it most. Perhaps we might think here of Jacques Lacan: 'the reason we go to poetry is not for wisdom, but for the dismantling of wisdom.'

Rather, the LFC's (not)-knowing is Utopian because it demands and confirms that the story is not over, and therefore that hope—a thing much contested—is undeniably extant. Do you remember Kevin Costner's *Postman*, who delivers not just mail but the thing with feathers to shacks across the scorched fields? Now we have Deliveroo and UberEATS; they keep the bought hope warm.

Who Watches from the Dark Porch, as Jorie Graham's poem advises us, will see things differently.

And yet... The LFC screen, like Fontana's slit, is open, door or window; and suitably in comes the wind (*'last night I couldn't sleep'*, Joni M confesses). Is it Ballard's *Wind from Nowhere* or Benjamin's storm of progress? Are our calamitous actions in the past gusting us there too fast, a landfill of carnage all around us? Or is it from the future—rushing in through the rent we have made in our contract with the natural, breaking the compact of mutual relation—to snatch us from the floor of our feet?

Do we look through it as Winston Smith did, escaping from torture into his dream of the 'golden country' far from *1984*? And yet, if we look at those trees on the hill, do we find them burning, trashed by an unknown hand?

We burn our fossil ancestors to destroy our descendants (film is oil).

We privilege exploitation of space / place at the expense of both those locations *and* time. Film is time *and* place in action.

What will this mean for the idea of a generative image? Collapse is known—its form is open, but its fact is not in doubt. We have said this before, and we will need to say it again.

The message is the bottle, and reverse. The candle pools within its own erasure—burn the whale at both ends, so they might have said.

What if there is no more unknown, just more of the bad known?

When an old road in the back lands is abandoned for a bypass in the glare, all that lived along the road dies with it— factories, towns, homesteads, farms: it's opioid time, again.

All of it is fractal. If I watch as a long-standing small business pulls down the shutters on its final trading day, I am also observing a city centre in decline, the nation's labour pursuing great migrations to the bunkers of the damned, the clear un-ravelling of the banks (plus siphon off of all our wealth into the private troughs), an iceberg calving in the southern seas and a single woman climbing stairs towards an attic bed, where she will lie down one last and long, long time, swallow deeply, lean back, close her eyes, between her folded hands a letter clear of time.

Production of concrete, metal, plastic, bricks and asphalt is now greater than the mass of living matter on the planet.

The world *we* have made will end the made world.

The LFC manifests here as 'late style' in and for a culture that is dying in real time, whatever that might be. It provides both the entropic rush into a point omega and the big bang of new origins that exist cyclically within the moment of dissolution.

When we consider that the most viewed images in human history come from *Baby Shark* (seen more times than the earth's population) and the until recently previously most watched are from a Latin lust song in which Luis Fonsi (operating in the opener as a kind of Puerto Rican Canute against the rising sea levels, which of course would wash the object—very much—of his desire away, and fast, not *despacito* as he would wish) wants nothing more than to follow 'the path' into the 'walls' of his beloved's 'labyrinth'—here less an Aleph than an Alpha male, and certainly an Ox tail—then we are left only with the sense that culture—as a medium or glue of transmission, of communal values, an ethical code, a foundation of priorities—has eaten itself like the Ouroboros of lore.

By this measure, *We're Going on a Bear Hunt* is an Odyssey quest towards self-realisation, *The Gruffalo* a veiled call for collective solidarity in the face of a fake news pandemic and *The Wheels on the Bus* as valid as *Land of Hope and Glory* in singing us together towards the shared national project; while actually what is happening is that white vans have become ambulances and funerals are taking place without mourners. But we should not worry so much—a people carrier is pulling up on country gravel as I type and a fashionably dressed man in late middle age, who has made his money from conning infants out of their pocket money via strategically placed algorithmic cookies, his silvered hair combed back, is unloading the boot and striding as satisfied as a cake into his detached villa.

In these first days of the last days, we need the compacted priority of prismatic vision resolving itself into access 'in real time,' a Ballardian diamonding of the very air itself, so that perception might both endure and deepen from inside the unscrolling crisis. As if we were able to narrate and circulate the experience of the car crash while it was crashing—a whole family dead on the A40 (not medically accurate; three children and a parent killed as one at once, while the remaining parent and child stutter and jolt on life support; would *you* want to wake out of that into such knowing?). But when did the accident begin? With the lorry and its heightened unseeing—he escaped with 'minor injuries'—or with the rain earlier on the glistening asphalt, or the sudden Autumnal dazzle through the pollarded trees, or the broken night's sleep as one of the four climbs aboard the great vessel of the double bed after a nightmare on the sea of troubled sleep, or on those four occasions when the children moved from idea to initiation, or when the garage missed the slackness of the brakes, or when they first glimpsed each other in the small town pub, drinking bitter shandy and dreaming of the city of the future, or when he was so angry he slammed the door to shake the walls and climbed into the cab, turning the talk radio so high he couldn't hear the traffic, or (or...or...or) when out of the great compressed void of entire being the pressure of emergence saw universal acceleration, a rushing forth as when blood under intolerable strain leaves the body to describe itself across the mourning road?

When something ends, when did that ending start? When 'they' no longer make what you like, what formed you, what aspired you, what you thought *was* meaning, true, itself? When the places you'd go to see the things you like are so altered, or erased, that their absence bleeds into your memory of, and experience within, the things they used to hold? When the people you shared these things with have left, have moved away or travelled even further, beyond reach of messages, and somehow now what once held value straggles like a husk, a hollow person, a torn and filthy shirt on a broomstick in Russian winds squalling over muddy Autumn fields...

There once was a time when the Trickster was so welcome —agitator, agent of upset, activist of riot in the spirit and the palace. No longer—the Joker, Holy Fool, has had the big house keys (still has them, many places). It's great when it's poetic, but in our lives, no thanks. Let's stick with the emperor being naked—on that we can agree. Why say this? Because the LFC is not a joke or gag, a prank or smug contrivance: it's as serious as breathing, trees or bees. It genuinely puts forward—it throws away the saw it's found lying on the branch. It does not operate at some remove but risks it all in saying: let's try this; all else let us down. The view from way above is not moral until it's closer —then you see the damage, you smell the charcoal woods. If you've got something at stake, stay close and fight for outcomes. The LFC doesn't deal results, but knows they might be out there, and can make informed assessments.

Have you asked of Siri or Alexa: is there a future out there worth the living? No, me neither yet. Better that we ask this of *ourselves*: we are history and so we are its children. It is not outside the door *or* in the room: it is everywhere. Gaze if you are lucky on the infinite tail of the bird-of-paradise. Evolution could make you mad with its brilliance, if you let it (David Attenborough might just have had the greatest life of any human who has ever lived) and why not, when the hour is so, so late? Given the mayfly lives for five minutes, given the nearest star would take 78,000 years to reach, what is to be done?

Light conspires with Earth to conceive potential. To reveal the leaves and squares, so sensually real, a solar sleight of hand that con / firms the body's true belief: it *is*.

The LFC implies a different mode of thinking about the future, one that can hold both extremes in mind and play.

(Loving film's circulation)

Ours is essentially a tragic age, so we refuse to take it tragically. The cataclysm has happened, we are among the ruins, we start to build up new little habitats, to have new little hopes. It is rather hard work: there is now no smooth road into the future: but we go round, or scramble over the obstacles. We've got to live, no matter how many skies have fallen.
    —D.H. Lawrence, from *Lady Chatterley's Lover*

You'll meet your destiny on the road you take to avoid it.
    —Carl Jung (quoting Jean de La Fontaine)

This essay is an afterword.

After words, what can be said (in the moment, from the moment) out of the gleaming moment?

We live in an age when hand sanitizer anticipates us; falls sometimes to the floor before the palm can nest it.

When is something—the world we loved and valued, say—no longer it itself? Yes, the human body, new cells every seven years etc. but I mean something more than just the actual.

This book is a manual of the possible film and therefore of the possible life / society / future. It operates, therefore, in the margins of the possible, with Mark Fisher's clean example keenly close (too missed, as all who are); that is, with a sharp nostalgia for the future we have lost, the retrieval of something that *has not happened yet...*

So, should we archive or should we not? Who are they for, the billions of photos, trillions of words? An inch in the final geology, they queue across the plains; await their great interring. There is no single answer, of course there never is, to the how, the why, the long what for.

Which is exactly why it makes the fullest sense this book has birthed—and berthed—with Tenement Press, sister in spirit and action to Close-Up's sweet prior hosting. Because... because 'a tenement is a type of building shared by multiple dwellings, typically with flats or apartments on each floor and with shared entrance stairway access...'

Yes, sincerely we all are, yes all of us who still are humble enough to be humane, on this voyage together. So, raise the sails, your canvas and your sticks, and let us all head out, from the harbour of the known, out across the open LFC...

*

The ultimate, hidden truth of the world is that it is something that we make and could just as easily make differently.
   —David Graeber (1961–2020), from *The Utopia of Rules: On Technology, Stupidity, and the Secret Joys of Bureaucracy* (2015)

*

... for here there is no place
that does not see you. You must change your life.
   —Rainer Maria Rilke, from *Archaic Torso of Apollo*

Gareth Evans does what he can.

MUSIC LISTENED TO IN THE WRITING OF THIS ESSAY—
Leyland Kirby, *We Drink to Forget the Coming Storm*
& *We, So Tired of All the Darkness in Our Lives*
    (you'll find them if you need them)

EATEN—Twiglets (£1 bags, 105 grams)

DRUNK—Yes (Bombay Sapphire Gin & Tonic in a can, £2.30)

EXERCISE—Haggerston Park woodland

MASK—Made by son's mother

DISTANCE—Too much

SLEEP—Not enough

HOMEWORK—Please read 'The Planet on the Table' by
Wallace Stevens; plant a tree

WORDS—5681

And now this is the END.

    8.3.21

Notes on Contributors
(In order of appearance)

Shezad Dawood works across film, painting and sculpture to juxtapose discrete systems of image, language, site and narrative, using the editing process as a method to explore meanings and forms between film and painting. His practice often involves collaboration, working with groups and individuals across different territories to physically and conceptually map far-reaching lines of enquiry. These networks chart different geographic locations and communities and are particularly concerned with acts of translation and re-staging.

Chris Petit is an internationally renowned author and filmmaker, once described by *Le Monde* as 'the Robespierre of English cinema.' His films include the definitive *Radio On* (1979) and have been the subject of several foreign retrospectives.

Andrea Luka Zimmerman is an artist, filmmaker and cultural activist whose engaged practice calls for a profound re-imagining of the relationship between people, place and ecology. Focusing on marginalised individuals, communities and experience, the practice employs imaginative hybridity and narrative re-framing, alongside reverie and a creative waywardness. Informed by suppressed histories, and alert to sources of radical hope, the work prioritises an enduring and equitable co-existence.

William Fowler is a film historian, writer, musician, and an archive curator at the BFI. His co-authored book *The Bodies Beneath: The Flipside of British Film and Television* was published by Strange Attractor Press in 2019. *blue thirty-three* by his band The Begotten is out on Blue Tapes; *Wire magazine* called it 'a great noisy slug.'

John Rogers is a writer and filmmaker based in London. He is the author of *This Other London—Adventures in the Overlooked City* (Harper Collins, 2013). He directed the feature documentaries *The London Perambulator* (2009), featuring Will Self, Iain Sinclair, Russell Brand, and Nick Papadimitriou; *Make Your Own Damn Art—the world of Bob and Roberta Smith* (2012), *London Overground* (2016) with Iain Sinclair, and *In the Shadow of the Shard* (2018). John was psychogeographer-in-residence for Waltham Forest London Borough of Culture 2019. He produces a regular series of videos on his YouTube channel.

Ben Rivers is a filmmaker, born in Somerset, lives in London. He has made over 40 films, with his first feature *Two Years at Sea* winning the International Critics Prize at 68th Venice Film Festival. Other awards include twice winning the Tiger Award at Rotterdam Film Festival, the Paul Hamlyn Foundation Award for Artists and the EYE Art Film Prize. He was commissioned by Artangel to make *The Two Eyes Are Not Brothers*, shown at the former BBC Television Centre and The Whitworth Museum, Manchester. Most recently he collaborated with Anocha Suwichakornpong on the feature film *Krabi*, 2562. He co-ran / programmed Brighton Cinematheque 1996–2006.

Gideon Koppel *"Born in London in 1960, and still looking for a place he'd like to die..."*

Gareth Evans is a London-based writer, curator, producer and presenter.

Adam Roberts—born in Bogota, Colombia—has made films and videos since the mid-90s. His film *Mickey Finn* won the Grand Prix du Jury at Angers international Film Festival. His collaborators have included film-maker Jack Hazan, choreographer Jonathan Burrows, composers Kevin Volans & Matteo Fargion, and the dancer Sylvie Guillem. His work has shown at Whitechapel Gallery, Hayward Gallery, Haus der Kunst, Munich, Maxi Gallery, Rome, and BFI Southbank. He produced and filmed an unprecedented series of interviews with long-term survivors of HIV (the AIDS Since the 80s Project, now The HIV Story Trust), housed in the London Metropolitan Archives, indexed and catalogued with support from the Wellcome Foundation. With Joanna Hogg he founded *A Nos Amours*, which has programmed screenings, curated exhibitions, and staged conferences. *A Nos Amours* has also published a book, the *Chantal Akerman Retrospective Handbook*, arising from a celebrated complete retrospective of Akerman's work at London's ICA. An exhibition at Ambika P3 of Akerman's installation work followed. His published writing includes chapters and journal papers, and the book *Lamentation—In the Stuart Croft Archive*, published by Ma Bibliothèque in 2020. Up to date information may be found at www.adamroberts.info.

John Akomfrah is an artist and filmmaker, whose works are characterised by their investigations into memory, post-colonialism, temporality and aesthetics and often explores the experiences of migrant diasporas globally. Akomfrah was a founding member of the influential Black Audio Film Collective, which started in London in 1982 alongside the artists David Lawson and Lina Gopaul, who he still collaborates with today. Their first film, *Handsworth Songs* (1986) explored the events surrounding the 1985 riots in Birmingham and London through a charged combination of archive footage, still photos and newsreel. The film won several international prizes and established a multi-layered visual style that has become a recognisable motif of Akomfrah's practice. Other works include *The Unfinished Conversation* (2012); *Peripeteia* (2012); *Mnemosyne* (2010); *Vertigo Sea* (2015); *Purple* (2017); *Precarity* (2017) and *Four Nocturnes* (2019).

Shama Khanna is an independent curator, writer and educator from London. They are the founder of Flatness (http:// flatness.eu), a long-running platform for artists' moving image and network culture invested in curating through a decolonial feminist lens. The project has been described as a 'digital site of resistance' (Dr Sylvia Theuri), decentring narratives of the arts and normalcy from the margins of the online. As well as with the artists featured on the site, Khanna has collaborated with numerous publications and organisations including: documenta 14, Athens; NANG, Seoul; Western Front, Vancouver; Microscope, NYC; *Art Monthly*; *Afterall*; LUX Scotland; Jerwood Arts; Herbert Gallery; Camden Arts Centre; The Women's Art Library, Goldsmiths; *Feminist Review Journal*; Chisenhale Gallery; Syllabus; and CCA, Glasgow (all UK). They are currently producing a Flatness book commissioned by Axisweb & Manchester Metropolitan University in partnership with the artist workers' co-operative not/nowhere. Khanna is a lecturer in Curating at the Royal College of Art, a Cultural Tenant at Studio Voltaire Studios, and a proud Trustee of not/nowhere.

Tony Grisoni worked in many different areas of film making before turning to screenwriting. *Queen of Hearts* (1989) was his award winning first feature directed by Jon Amiel. He has worked closely with a number of directors including Michael Winterbottom, John Boorman, Sean Durkin and Marc Munden, and has co-written with Terry Gilliam, including *Fear & Loathing in Las Vegas* (1998); *Tideland* (2005) and that ship of fools, *The Man Who Killed Don Quixote* (2018). Other works include *In this World* (2001); *Brothers of the Head* (2005); *Red Riding* (2009); *The Unloved* (2009); *Southcliffe* (2013); *The Young Pope* (2016); *Crazy Diamond* (2017); and *The City and the City* (2018).

Damien Sanville is the founder of Close-Up Film Centre.

Mania Akbari is an internationally acclaimed artist and film-maker. Her provocative, revolutionary and radical films were recently the subject of retrospectives at the BFI, London (2013), the DFI, Denmark (2014), Oldenburg International Film Festival, Germany (2014), Cyprus Film Festival (2014) and Nottingham Contemporary UK (2018). Her films have screened at festivals around the world and have received numerous awards including German Independence Honorary Award, Oldenberg (2014), Best Film, Digital Section, Venice Film Festival (2004), Nantes Special Public Award Best Film (2007) and Best Director and Best film at Kerala Film Festival (2007), Best Film and Best Actress, Barcelona Film Festival (2007). Akbari was exiled from Iran and currently lives and works in London, a theme addressed in *Life May Be* (2014), co-directed with Mark Cousins. This film was released at Karlovy Vary Film Festival and was nominated for Best Documentary at Edinburgh International Film Festival (2014) and Asia Pacific Film Festival (2014). Akbari's latest film *A Moon For My Father*, made in collaboration with British artist Douglas White, premiered at CPH:DOX where it won the NEW:VISION Award 2019. The film also received a FIPRESCI International Critics Award at the Flying Broom Festival, Ankara.

Xiaolu Guo is a Chinese / British filmmaker and novelist. She has directed 11 films, including features *How Is Your Fish Today* (2007) and *UFO In Her Eyes* (2011). Her fiction *She A Chinese* received the Golden Leopard award at the Locarno Film Festival 2009. She self-produced all her documentaries. *Once Upon A Time Proletarian* (2011) premiered at the Venice Film Festival, *We Went to Wonderland* (2008) premiered at the MOMA in New York, and *Five Men & A Caravaggio* (2018) premiered at the BFI London Film Festival. She has had film retrospectives at the Whitechapel Gallery in London (2019); Swiss Cinematheque (2010); and Greek Film Archives (2018). Her memoir, *Once Upon A Time in The East* won the National Book Critics Circle Award, 2017 and *A Lover's Discourse* is her most recent novel.

Sean Price Williams is a New York-based cinematographer, known for producing some of the most colourful and thrilling images in independent cinema today. He shoots both film and digital across categories of narrative, documentary, and experimental cinema. Some of Williams' notable recent credits include *Her Smell* (2018); *Marjorie Prime* (2017); and *Good Time* (2017).

Chloe Aridjis is the author of three novels, *Book of Clouds* (2009), which won the Prix du Premier Roman Etranger in France, *Asunder* (2013), set in London's National Gallery, and *Sea Monsters* (2019), recently awarded the PEN / Faulkner Award for Fiction. Aridjis has written for various art journals and was a guest curator at Tate Liverpool. She stars in Josh Appignanesi's psychodrama *Female Human Animal* (2018) and received a Guggenheim Fellowship in 2014. Chloe is a member of XR Writers Rebel, a group of writers who focus on addressing the climate emergency, and dreams of a world in which animals cease to be exploited.

Athina Tsangari is a Greek director and producer. Her first work in cinema was in a small acting role in Richard Linklater's *Slacker* (1991). She went on to produce work by Linklater, as well as that of Yorgos Lanthimos. She is best known for directing the feature films *The Slow Business of Going* (2000); *Attenberg* (2010); and *Chevalier* (2016).

Juliet Jacques is a writer and filmmaker based in London, UK. *Trans: A Memoir* (2015), was published by Verso, and her most recent book, *Variations* (2021), was published by Influx Press. Her short fiction, essays and journalism have appeared in numerous publications, and her short films have screened in galleries and festivals worldwide. She hosts the podcast *Suite (212)*, which looks at the arts in their social, cultural, political and historical contexts.

Anna Thew is a painter turned filmmaker, writer and performer. Her work has been screened and celebrated literally everywhere.

Adam Christensen is a London-based artist who makes performance, video, fabric and text works, and performs with the music project Ectopia, which was Wysing Arts Centre's band-in-residence in 2016. He has previously performed and presented work at Overgaden Institute for Contemporary Art; Copenhagen Baltic Triennial; as well as Almanac; David Roberts Art Foundation; Southard Reid; Institute of Contemporary Arts (London); Hollybush Gardens; Goldsmiths CCA (London).

Laura Mulvey is Professor of Film at Birkbeck College, University of London. She is the author of *Visual and Other Pleasures* (Macmillan, 1989 / 2009); *Fetishism and Curiosity* (British Film Institute, 1996 / 2013); *Citizen Kane* (bfi Classics series, 1992 / 2012); *Death Twenty-four Times a Second: Stillness and the Moving Image* (Reaktion Books, 2006) and *Afterimages: on Cinema, Women and Changing Times* (Reaktion Books, 2019) as well as three co-edited collections of essays. She made six films in collaboration with Peter Wollen, including *Riddles of the Sphinx* (1977) and *Frida Kahlo and Tina Modotti* (1980). With artist / filmmaker Mark Lewis, she made *Disgraced Monuments* (1994) and *23 August 2008* (2013).

Astra Taylor is a writer, documentary filmmaker, and activist. Her films include *Zizek!* (2005); *Examined Life* (2008), and *What Is Democracy?* (2018). Her books include *The People's Platform* (2014) and *Democracy May Not Exist But We'll Miss it When It's Gone* (2019) and, as co-editor, *Occupy! Scenes from Occupied America* (2011). She is a Fellow of the Shuttleworth Foundation for her work against predatory debt.

Dennis Cooper is the author of nine novels as well as numerous books of poetry and non-fiction. He has made two feature films in collaboration with artist Zac Farley, *Permanent Green Light* (2018) and *Like Cattle Towards Glow* (2015). His most recent publications are a novel, *The Marbled Swarm* (2011) and four works of fiction composed of animated gifs, most recently the gif novel *Zac's Freight Elevator* (2016) and a short gif fiction collection, *Zac's Coral Reef* (2018). He has written the works of French theatre director and choreographer Gisele Vienne since 2004. He has recently completed his tenth novel, *I Wished*, and is currently working on *Room Temperature*, his third film with Farley. He lives in Paris and Los Angeles. See also, denniscooperblog.com.

Stewart Home, author, is the only person on earth who is visible to the naked eye from outer space. He really does burn that brightly. *The London Review of Books* has praised Home by saying: "I really don't think anyone who is at all interested in literature has any business not knowing the work of Stewart Home." However, this notorious egg bagel eater prefers to liken himself to "a proletarian comedian with Tourette's spewing obscenities." Home much prefers standing on his head and reciting sexually explicit passages from his work at public events to courting the literary establishment, but nonetheless Home has recently published *Re-Enter the Dragon: Genre Theory, Brucesploitation & the Sleazy Joys of Lowbrow Cinema* (2018); and, previously, *Blood Rites of the Bourgeoisie* (2010); *Sixty-Nine Things To Do With A Dead Princess* (2002); *Slow Death* (1996); and *The Easy Way to Falsify Your Credit Rating* (2005), to name but a few.

Dan Fox is a writer, filmmaker and musician living in New York, USA. He is the author of the books *Limbo* (2018) and *Pretentiousness: Why It Matters* (2016).

Miranda Pennell originally trained in contemporary dance and later studied visual anthropology. Pennell has produced a body of award-winning film and video work that explores forms of collective performance, whether dancers, soldiers or fight directors. Her most recent moving-image work uses colonial archives as the starting point for investigations into the colonial imaginary. Pennell's films include *You Made Me Love You* (2005); *Tattoo* (2001); *Fisticuffs* (2004); *Why Colonel Bunny Was Killed* (2010); and *The Host* (2015).

Elena Gorfinkel is a senior lecturer in film studies at King's College London and the author of *Lewd Looks: American Sexploitation Cinema in the 1960s* (2017). Her criticism appears in *Sight & Sound*, *Art Monthly*, and *Cinema Scope*, among other publications.

Tai Shani is a Tutor in Contemporary Art Practice at the Royal College of Art. Shani's multidisciplinary practice, comprising performance, film, photography, and installation, revolves around experimental narrative texts. Shani recently published *Our Fatal Magic* (2019)—a work of feminist science fiction that anticipates a post-patriarchal future.

Stephen Watts is a poet & translator. Among recent books are *Ancient Sunlight* (2014) and *Gramsci & Caruso* (2014), a selected poems with Italian translation by Cristina Viti. *Republic of Dogs / Republic of Birds*—written on a typewriter in the late 1980s, then mislaid, lost, and found again in 2012—was first published by Test Centre and recently reissued by Prototype, 2020. A feature-length 16mm black-and-white film based on *The Republics* was made in 2019 by filmmaker Huw Wahl.

Stanley Schtinter has been described as an 'artist' by the *Daily Mail*—as an 'exorcist' by the *Daily Star*.

The Liberated Film Club
Stanley Schtinter, *et al*

Grisoni's references to Tony Garnett's memoir, *The Day the Music Died: A Life Behind the Lens* (Constable, 2016), are iterations of Garnett's prose altered slightly in their live recitation; Williams' referral to Whistler's 'Ten O'clock Lecture' (1885)—an hour-long address on art and art making delivered to an assembly of London based artists, dealers, and members of the press—is a brief excerpt from the *Correspondences of James McNeill Whistler* made available to the public via digital concordance by the University of Glasgow, School of Culture and Creative Arts. Sahba Shayani's translation of Hafez's 'Ghazal 360' appears in this volume for the first time; the editors are grateful to Elhum Shakerifar for her assistance and support with this commission. The accompanying photographic reproductions of the Hafez are the artist's own, © Mania Akbari, 2021.

Stickered editions feature a photograph lifted from the *Glasgow Herald*, 1957, 'Men watching fire crews tackle a blaze at Riverside Mills through the night.'

The images of 'FIRE' assembled in this edition were contributed by attendees of the Liberated Film Club following a special request from this edition's editor, Stanley Schtinter. pp.vii, xi, xiv, 24, 32, 40, 50, 80, 174, 179 and 318 are reproduced with kind permission and exclusive arrangement with *Augenblick* ('a journal dedicated to the art of the anonymous photograph'); and pp.260, 278 and 288 are excerpted from Louis Benassi's personal archive of found film. Additional images of fire were contributed by the 'END TIME HEALERS,' Stewart Home; Dan Fox; Cody Brant; Alxnot; Francis Macpherson; Maria Anastassiou; and Raminta Uselyte. The images accompanying the contributions from Anna Thew ('A Train in the Night Passing'), Tai Shani ('Outsides and Erotics'), and Stanley Schtinter ('A Letter from the Curator') are the artist's own, © 2021. The photographs in Elena Gorfinkel's segment ('The Last Things Before the Last') are excerpted from *Coming Apart* (1969) by Milton Moses Ginsberg. The (impossible) film stills are excerpted from commissioned posters designed exclusively for the Liberated Film Club series by Traven T. Croves, and (possibly) owe to such filmmakers as György Fehér; Cecilia Mangini; Chris Petit; Ula Stöckl; John Samson; Salah Abouseif; Romain Gary; Svetlana Proskurina; Yuri Ilyenko; Andrzej Czarnecki; and Pedro Olea. A selection of films from which these images (may) have been drawn have been programmed to mark this publication and will be made publicly accessible for free (and in perpetuity), exclusively at Close-Up Film Centre, London. For further information on the films and programme, address all enquiries for the attention of Stanley Schtinter at 97 Sclater Street, London E1 6HR. For access to the Close-Up Film Centre library, contact the venue.

A final, additional thanks goes to the bar staff at Close-Up, PAX, and—by way of Jake Wardle—recommend a toast (to Louis Benassi): one-part single malt whisky; two-parts bourbon; one-part lemon juice; a dash of bitters; and a dash or two of syrup (specifically, from the virtually untouched and several-years-old jar of Maraschino cherries on the shelf). To be shaken and served over rocks.

A CIP record for this publication is available from the
British Library.

Tenement Press 2, MMXXI
ISBN 978-1-8380200-3-3

Printed and bound by Lulu.
Typeset in Arnhem Pro Blond, Geeza Pro & Hiragino Sans.

Tenement Press is an occasional publisher of esoteric;
experimental;
accidental;
and interdisciplinary literatures.

www.tenementpress.com
editors@tenementpress.com